THE ART AND MEANING OF MAGIC

SMALL GEMS BY
DR. ISRAEL REGARDIE

Some Other Titles From New Falcon Publications

Aha! The Sevenfold Mystery of the Ineffable Love — **By Aleister Crowley**
Bio-Etheric Healing — **By Trudy Lanitis**
Undoing Yourself With Energized Meditation and Other Devices
Secrets of Western Tantra: The Sexuality of the Middle Path
Dogma Daze — **By Christopher S. Hyatt, Ph.D.**
Rebels & Devils; The Psychology of Liberation **Edited by Christopher S. Hyatt, Ph.D.**
Aleister Crowley's Illustrated Goetia
Taboo: Sex, Religion & Magick
Sex Magic, Tantra & Tarot: The Way of the Secret Lover
 — **By Christopher S. Hyatt, Ph.D., and Lon Milo DuQuette**
Pacts With The Devil
Urban Voodoo: A Beginner's Guide to Afro-Caribbean Magic
 — **By Jason Black and Christopher S. Hyatt, Ph.D.**
The Psychopath's Bible — **By Christopher S. Hyatt, Ph.D., and Jack Willis**
Ask Baba Lon — **By Lon Milo DuQuette**
Aleister Crowley and the Treasure House of Images **By J.F.C. Fuller, Aleister Crowley, Lon Milo DuQuette and Nancy Wasserman**
Enochian World of Aleister Crowley **By Lon Milo DuQuette and Aleister Crowley**

Info-Psychology   Neuropolitique   The Game of Life
What Does WoMan Want? — **By Timothy Leary, Ph.D.**

Be Yourself - A Guide to Relaxation and Health
Dr. Israel Regardie's Definitive Work on Aleister Crowley, The Eye In The Triangle
Healing Energy, Prayer and Relaxation
My Rosicrucian Adventure
Teachers of Fulfillment
The Complete Golden Dawn System of Magic
The Eye in the Triangle: An Interpretation of Aleister Crowley
The Golden Dawn Audio CDs
The Legend of Aleister Crowley
The Portable Complete Golden Dawn System of Magic
The Tree of Life
What You Should Know About the Golden Dawn — **By Dr. Israel Regardie**

Roll Away The Stone/The Herb Dangerous **By Israel Regardie and Aleister Crowley**

Rebellion, Revolution and Religiousness — **By Osho**
Reichian Therapy: A PracticalGuide for Home Use — **By Dr. Jack Willis**
Woman's Orgasm: A Guide to Sexual Satisfaction — **By Benjamin Graber, M.D., and Georgia Kline-Graber, R.N.**
Shaping Formless Fire   Seizing Power   Taking Power — **By Stephen Mace**
The Illuminati Conspiracy: The Sapiens System — **By Donald Holmes, M.D.**
The Secret Inner Order Rituals of the Golden Dawn — **By Pat Zalewski**

MANY OF OUR TITLES AVAILABLE ON KINDLE!
Please visit our website at http://www.newfalcon.com

THE ART AND MEANING OF MAGIC

SMALL GEMS BY
DR. ISRAEL REGARDIE

NEW FALCON PUBLICATIONS
LAS VEGAS, NEVADA, U.S.A.

Copyright © 2018 New Falcon Publications

All rights reserved. No part of this book,
in part or in whole, may be reproduced, transmitted,
or utilized, in any form or by any means, electronic or mechanical,
including photocopying, recording, or by any information storage
and retrieval system, without permission in writing
from the publisher, except for brief quotations
in critical articles, books and reviews.

ISBN 13: 978-1-56184-555-2
ISBN 10: 1-56184-555-8

New Falcon Publications First Edition 2018

The paper used in this publication meets the minimum requirements
of the American National Standard for Permanence of
Paper for Printed Library Materials Z39.48-1984

Printed in USA

NEW FALCON PUBLICATIONS
9550 South Eastern Avenue • Suite 253
Las Vegas, NV 89123
www.newfalcon.com
email: info@newfalcon.com

CONTENTS

Magic in East and West	1
The Art of Magic	39
The Meaning of Magic	71
Bibliographical Note	101

MAGIC IN EAST AND WEST

When I was about seventeen years of age, a friend loaned me a copy of Major L.A. Waddell's *Lamaism*. In those days it impressed me tremendously, no doubt because of its massive size. In every sense it was a heavy tome, and tomes then suggested depth and weight of scholarship and insight. Naturally I knew nothing at that time about Magic, and beyond a few theosophical allusions next to nothing of Buddhism. So the greater part of the significance and wide erudition of the book must have passed me by completely, though it is a veritable storehouse of knowledge.

Then, out of the blue it appeared on my horizon again, again through the agency of a friend. In the light of the little knowledge and experience gained through the passage of several years, its contents excited me enormously–and it was with the utmost interest that I reconsidered it. For me, one of the things that stood out most emphatically this time was the extraordinary similarity between–even the fundamental unity of–the highest and most basic magical conceptions of both East and West. Whether this is due, as many exponents of the Eastern wisdom would claim, to the direct importation of occult philosophy and practice from the Orient to Western civilization, it is not my intention now to argue. Nonetheless, it is my considered belief that in Occidental countries there has definitely been a secret tradition on a practical level–a tradition which for centuries has orally transmitted the finer part of this magical knowledge. In fact, so jealously reserved at all times was this tradition that by most people it was hardly suspected at all. Very few were the fortunate individuals who in any age were drawn as though by individuals who in any age were drawn as though by invisible currents of spiritual affinity to the concealed portals of its temples.

Occasionally a small portion of this closely concealed tradition wormed it way outwards into books. Some of these latter are those which were written by Iamblichus and the later Neoplatonists, and also by students such as Cornelius Agrippa, Pietro d'Albano and Eliphas Levi, etc. Its cruder elements found expression in the far-famed Clavicles, Grimoires and Goetias. Yet for the most part its practical knowledge were, as above stated, maintained in strict privacy. The reason for this secrecy may have been the feeling that there are only a small number in any age, in any country, amongst any people who are likely to appreciate or understand the deeper or sublimer aspects of Theurgy, the higher magic. It requires sympathy, much insight and a capacity for hard work, which needless to say few people possess. And there is, consequently, but little point scattering broadcast these pearls of bright wisdom which can only be misunderstood.

Indubitably this conclusion is corroborated by Waddell's *Lamaism*. In point of fact, a good deal of so-called esoteric magical knowledge is there contained–though it is presented wholly without comprehension. Hence his statement of that particular aspect of Lamaism is vitiated and rendered practically worthless. And while I may agree with Waddell that some of the Lamaistic practices have little to do with historical Buddhism, his sneers as regards to esoteric Buddhism on the magical side of things are simply laughable, for his own book is a clear demonstration of precisely that one fact which he has perceived not at all.

His book, obviously, was intended primarily to be an objective account of the Buddhism indigenous to Tibet and as practised by its monks and hermits. Unfortunately, the prejudices and misunderstandings of the author are scarcely concealed. So that while indubitably he did pick up some of the crumbs dropped haphazard from the esoteric table of the Lamas, and recorded them probably as he found them, nevertheless he had not the necessary training, knowledge or insight into the subject possessed undoubtedly by some of the higher initiated Lamas with whom he had conversed. The result was that he was unable to make anything of that information. In fact, *his* account of their practices sounds simply silly and absurd. Psychologically, he succeeds not in throwing ridicule on the Lamas but only upon himself.

Certain aspects of Theurgy or Western Magic have now been comparatively clearly set forth. Some early reviewers and critics were of the opinion that my former work *The Tree of Life* was as plain an elementary statement of its major traditional principles as had yet publicly been made. And Dion Fortune's book *The Mystical Qabalah*, a frank masterpiece, is likewise an incomparably fine rendition of the mystical philosophy that underlies the practice of Magic. I therefore suggest that by employing the theorems laid down in those two books, and applying them to the material in Waddell's *Lamaism*, we may arrive at an understanding of some otherwise obscure portions of Tibetan Magic.

It may be well, at first, to confess that a good part of the magical routine refers to a psychic plane, to certain levels of the Collective Unconscious, though by no means does that wholly condemn it as certain mystical schools feel inclined to do. Other branches concern such phenomenal accomplishments as rain-making, obtaining good crops, scaring away demons, and similar feats with which both Eastern and Occidental legend have familiarised us. Feats, moreover, which require a good deal of explaining away by the rationalist and mechanistic scientist. Finally, there is that unhappily large part which verges on witchcraft pure and simple. With this latter, I am at no time concerned. But I maintain, as a primal definition, that Magic whether of the Eastern or Western variety, is essentially a divine process–Theurgy, a mode of spiritual culture or development. From the psychological viewpoint, it may be interpreted as a series of techniques having as their object the withdrawal of energy from objective and subjective objects so that, in the renewal of consciousness by a re-emergent libido, the jewel of a transformed life with new creative possibilities and with spontaneity may be found. It comprises various technical methods, some simple in nature, others highly complex and most difficult to perform, for purifying the personality, and into that cleaned organism freed of pathogenic strain invoking the higher Self. With this in mind, then, a good many of the apparently unrelated items of Magic, some of its invocations and visualising practices, take on a new and added significance. They are important psychological steps whereby to repair, improve or elevate consciousness so that eventually it may prove a worthy vehicle of the Divine Light. A sentence or two written many years ago by William Quan Judge in his pamphlet *An Epitome of Theosophy* express so exactly the impression to be conveyed that it is convenient to quote: "The real object to be kept in view is to so open up or make porous the lower nature that the spiritual nature may shine through it and become the guide and ruler. It is only 'cultivated' in the sense of having a vehicle prepared for its use, into which is may descend."

This conception is likewise the point of view of our magical system. The technical forms of Magic described in *The Golden Dawn*, such as Pentagram and other rituals, astral assumption of God-forms, evocations (though not necessarily to physical manifestation) of elemental and planetary spirits, skrying in the spirit-vision, and the invocation of the Holy Guardian Angel, are all performed with that single objective held ever before one. Theurgy and the exponents of the Eastern mysticisms are thus in complete accord on the fundamental theoretical principles.

To illustrate now what I mean by the complete misunderstanding which is a purely objective account of magical practices is capable of achieving, it will be found interesting to consider but a few statements made by Waddell. First of all, let me quote from page 152 (2nd edition) of his work: "The purest Ge-lug-pa Lama was awaking every morning, and before venturing outside his room, fortifies himself against assault by the demons by first of all assuming the spiritual guise of his fearful tutelary...Thus when the Lama emerges from his room...he presents spiritually the appearance of the demon-king, and the smaller malignant demons, being deluded into the belief that the Lama is indeed their own vindictive king, they flee from his presence, leaving the Lama unharmed."

Surely this is a puerile interpretation. Though the fact itself of the assumption of the spiritual forms of tutelary deities is perfectly correct, the rationale he provides is infantile and stupid. So far as Western Theurgy is concerned, centuries of effort have shown that one of the most potent adjuncts to spiritual experience, as aiding the assimilation of the lower self into the all-inclusive psyche, is the astral assumption of the magical form of a divine Force or a God. By means of an exaltation of the mind and soul to its presence, whilst giving utterance to an invocation, it is conceded that there may be a descent of the Light into the heart of the devotee, accompanied *pari passu* by an ascent of the mind towards the ineffable splendour of the spirit.

So far as the reason for and explanation of this process is concerned, it may be well to state briefly that according to the magical hypothesis, the whole cosmos is permeated and vitalised by One omnipresent Life, which in itself is both immanent as well as transcendent. At the dawn of the manifestation of the universe from the thrice unknown darkness, there issue forth the Lives–great gods and spiritual forces, *Cosmocratores*, who become the intelligent architects and builders of the manifold parts of the universe. From their own individual spiritual essence, other lesser hierarchies are begotten, and these in turn emanate or evolve from themselves still other groups. These are they which represent in the hidden depths of the psyche those primordial ideas which Jung speaks of as archetypal images ever present in the Collective Unconscious of the race. Thus it is that through the union of the human consciousness with the being of the gods in an ascending scale that the soul of man may gradually approach the final root and source of his being. In the Buddhist scheme this is "the essence of mind which is intrinsically pure," the Dharmakaya, the unconditioned divine body of truth. The intent to frighten malignant demons has no inclusion within the scope of this technique. Whether the later hypothesis is original with Major Waddell or not is difficult to surmise, though the thesis is common to all primitive peoples. Probably it was made by a Lama in a higher vein to put an end to leading questions; though at the same time it is true that in moments of psychic danger, the assumption of a God-form is of enormous assistance. Not because the threatening elemental or demon, for example, is fooled or frightened by the form. But because the operator, in opening himself to one phase of the divine spirit by the assumption of its symbolic form, does take upon himself or is empowered with the authority and dominion of that God.

It was in Egypt, so far as the western for of magic is concerned, that these cosmic forces received close attention and their qualities and attributes observed and recorded. Thus arose the conventionalised pictographs of their Gods which are profound in significance, while simple in the moving eloquence of their description. It is the Egyptian God-forms that are used in occidental magic, not those of Tibet or India. The technical use of these God-forms consists in the application of the powers of will and imagination–as well as of sound and colour. A very profound paragraph may be found in *The Mahatma Letters*, where K. H. wrote to A. P. Sinnett: "How could you make yourself understood–command in fact those semi-intelligent forces, whose means of communicating with us are not through spoken words but through sounds and colours, in correlations between the vibrations of the two. For sound, light and colour are the main factors in forming these grades of intelligence..."

Though it is hardly politic to enter more deeply into this manner, the remarks of K. H. apply equally to other forces and powers than elemental. The astral form of colour and light assumed in the imagination creates a mould or a focus of a special kind into which, by technical modes of vibration and invocation, the force or spiritual power desired incarnates. By the clothing of one's own astral form with the ideal figure of the God, now vitalised by the descent of the invoked force, it is held that man may be assumed or exalted into the very bosom of God-head, and so gradually return, with the acquisition of his own humanity, to that unnameable mysterious Root wherefrom originally he came.

Another instance of Waddell's lack of humour and insight occurs on page 322. In describing the training of the novice, it is said that the Lama adopts a "deep hoarse voice, acquired by training in order to convey the idea that it emanates from maturity and wisdom." It is not known to me whether any of my readers have witnessed any kind of a magical ceremony, or heard an invocation recited by a skilled practitioner–though I should say few have. The tone always adopted is one which will yield the maximum of vibration. For many students a deep intoning, or a humming, is the one which vibrates the most. Therefore that is the ideal tone whereby to awaken from within the subtle magical forces required. It will have been noted too that the best invocations are always sonorous and intensely vibrant. The idea that the voice should suggest maturity and wisdom is merely silly. This is another instance of Western contempt rather than a sympathetic attempt really to understand a foreign system. The Tibetan specimens of ritual given by Waddell contain an amusing number of Oms, Hums, Has, and Phats, but then Western conjurations contain equally amusing barbarous names of evocation. Yah, Agla, etc.

With this question of sound in magical conjurations I have dealt at some length elsewhere. Suffice to remark here that in *The Secret Doctrine* Madame Blavatsky suggests that the vibratory use of conjurations and sound generally have a profound significance. "Sound and rhythm," she observes, "are closely related to the four elements...Such or another vibration in the air is sure to awaken corresponding powers, union with which produces good or bad results, as the case may be." The whole subject of sound, and the employment of so-called barbarous names of evocation, requires thoroughly to be studied before one dare suggest an explanation accusing either Magi or Lamas merely of a pose of wisdom.

One notes with aroused attention too that the Tibetans have a form of what is called here in the Occident the Qabalistic Cross. On page 432 of his book, there is the following description: "Before commencing any devotional exercise, the higher Lamas perform or go through a manoeuvre bearing a close resemblance to 'crossing oneself' as practised by Christians. The Lama gently touches his forehead either with the finger or with the bell, uttering the mystic Om, then he touches the top of his chest, uttering Ah, then the epigastrium (pit of stomach) uttering Hum. And some Lamas add Sva-ha, while others complete the cross by touching the left shoulder, uttering Dam and then Yam. It is alleged that the object of these manipulations is to concentrate the parts of the Sattva, namely the body, speech, and mind upon the image or divinity which he is about to commune with."

Prior to commenting upon the above, it is imperative to indicate certain fundamental theories to be found in some books of the Qabalah. If the reader is familiar with Dr. Wm. W. Westcott's splendid *Introduction to the Study of the Kabballah* or with Dion Fortune's more recent book *The Mystical Qabalah* he will have seen there a diagram attributing the Ten Sephiroth to the figure of a man. Above the head, forming a crown, is *Keser* which represents the divine spirit, and at the feet is *Malkus*, while to the right

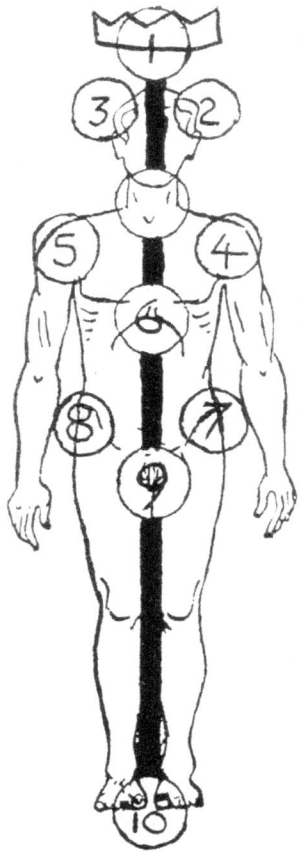

In the diagram of the Ten Sephiroth as applied to man above, the numbers given refer to the Sephiros as follows: 1–Keser; 2–Chockmah; 3–Binah; 4–Gedulah; 5–Gevurah; 6–Tiphares; 7–Netzach; 8–Hod; 9–Yesod; 10–Malkus. The one left blank at the throat is Daas.

and left shoulders are attributed *Gevurah* and *Gedulah*, Mars and Jupiter, Power and Majesty. In Qabalistic pneumatology, *Keser* is a correspondence of the Monad, the dynamic and essential self-hood of a man, the spirit which seeks experience through incarnation here on earth. That this Sephirah or potency is placed above the head rather than, say, within the brain or in the centre of the heart, is highly significant. It is the light of the Spirit which shines always into the darkness below. ("The spirit of man is the candle of the Lord." And again, "When his candle shined upon my head and by his light I walked through darkness.") This is an idea which has its parallels in other systems too. For example, in *The Epitome of Theosophy* we find Judge writing: "It is held that the real man, who is the higher self, being the spark of the Divine, overshadows the visible being, which has the possibility of becoming united to that spark. Thus it is said that the higher Spirit is not in the man, but above him."

All mystical and magical procedure has as its object so to purify the lower self that this higher Self which normally only overshadows us and is seldom in full incarnation, may descend into a purified and consecrated vehicle. The theurgic tradition asserts that, by the proper performance of the Qabalistic Cross amongst other things this end may be accomplished. As a devotional exercise or meditation, it is

used in collaboration with the formulation of certain lineal figures, the vibration of names of power, and followed by the invocation of the four great archangels. Its western form is as follows:
1. Touch the forehead, and say *Atoh* (Thou art)
2. Touch the breast, say *Malkus* (the Kingdom)
3. Touch the right shoulder, say *ve-Gevurah* (and the Power)
4. Touch the left shoulder, say *ve-Gedulah* (and the Glory)
5. Clasping the hands over the heart, say *le-Olahm, Amen* (for ever, Amen.)
6. Here follow suitable Pentagrams made facing the cardinal quarters, and the vibration of names of power.
7. Extend the arms in the form of a cross, saying:
8. Before me Raphael, Behind me Gabriel.
9. On my right hand Michael, on my left hand Auriel.
10. For before me flames the Pentagram.
11. And behind me shines the six-rayed Star.
12. Repeat 1-5, the Qabalistic Cross.

So far as this little ritual is concerned, one may describe its action as under several heads. It first invokes the power of the higher Self as a constant source of surveillance and guidance. It places the subsequent procedures under the divine aegis. Having then banished by the tracing of the appropriate pentagrams all non-essential beings from the four cardinal points with the aid of the four four-lettered names of God, it then calls the four Archangels–the four concretized functions of the interior psychic world, and the dual pair of opposites–to protect the sphere of magical operation, that is the circle of the Self. In closing, it once again invokes the higher Self, so that from the beginning to the end, the entire ceremony is under the guardianship of the spirit. The first section, comprising points one to five, identifies the higher Self of the operator with the highest aspects of the Sephirotic universe. In fact, it affirms the soul's essential identity with the collective consciousness of the whole of mankind.

If one attempted a further analysis, the Hebrew Word Atoh, meaning "Thou", would refer to the divine white brilliance, the higher Self overshadowing each man. By drawing down the Light to the pit of the stomach–which symbolically represents the feet, since to bend down to the feet would make an awkward gesture–the vertical shaft of a cross of Light is established in the imagination. The horizontal shaft is affirmed by touching both the shoulders, and vibrating words which state that the qualities of the higher self include both power and majesty, severity and lovingkindness. Equilibrium is the especial characteristic of the cross as a particular symbol, and the tracing of the Qabalistic Cross within the aura affirms the descent of the spirit and its equilibrium within consciousness or within the magical sphere. This meaning is further emphasised by the gesture of clasping the hands over the *Tipharas* centre, the heart place of harmony and balance, and saying *le-Olahm, Amen*, forever.

The Sanskrit word *Sattva* implies purity and rhythm and harmony, and of the three Gunas or qualities refers to Spirit. Similarly in the Western equivalent of this schema. Alchemy, the three qualities are correspondences of the three major Alchemical principles, Salt, Sulphur and Mercury. Of these the Universal Mercury is an attribution of *Keser*–that holy angel who is the divine guardian and Watcher, overshadowing the soul of man, ever awaiting an ordered approach so that its vehicle may be lifted up to its own glory. There is here, then, a very great resemblance between the Tibetan devotional exercise and that which is enjoined as one of the most important practices of the Qabalistic Magic of the Occidental tradition.

In that section of the book where Waddell describes the Lamaistic celebration of the Eucharist, another important parallelism is to be found. It describes how the priest or lama who conducts the ceremony is obliged to have purified himself during the greater part of the preceding twenty four hours by ceremonial bathing, and by having uplifted his mind through continual repetition of mantras or invocations. The actual description of the inner or magical aspect of the ritual, while not particularly well stated, is given for what it is worth: "Everything being ready and the congregation assembled, the priest, ceremonially pure by the ascetic rites above noted, and dressed in robe and mantle, abstracts from the great image of the Buddha *Amitayus* part of the divine essence of that deity, by placing the *vajra* of his *rdor jehi t'ag* upon the nectar vase which the image of *Amitayus* holds in his lamp, and applying the other end to his own bosom, over his heart. Thus, through the string, as by a telegraph wire passes the divine spirit, and the Lama must mentally conceive that his heart is in actual union with that of the god *Amitayus* and that, for the time being, he is himself that god."

After this meditation, the rice-offerings and the fluid in a special vase are consecrated by very "fierce" invocations and cymbal music. Then the consecrated food and water is partaken of by the assembly.

From the theurgic viewpoint the rationale of the Eucharist is quite simple. There may be innumerable types of Eucharist, all having different ends in view. A substance is chosen having a special affinity according to the doctrine of sympathies for a particular kind of spiritual force or god and ceremonially consecrated. Thus a wheaten wafer is of the substance of the Corn-goddess, attributed either to the powers of Venus, or to the element of Earth, presided over by Ceres or Persephone. Penetrative oils would be specially referred to the element of Fire, the tutelary deity of which is Horus. Olives would be sacred to the force represented by the astrological sign Aquarius, the element Air, and the goddess Hathor. And wine is referred to Dionysius and the solar gods generally, Osiris, Ra, etc. By an elaborate table of correspondences it is possible to select any substance to be the physical basis for the manifestation of a spiritual idea. The consecration, ceremonially, of the material basis by means of an invocation of the divine force accomplishes what is vulgarly called the miracle of transsubstantiation. To use more preferable magical terminology, the substance is transformed from a dead inert body into a living organism, a talisman in short. The consecration charges it and gives it a soul, as it were.

At this juncture, I must register my emphatic disagreement with those writers on science and Magic who, impressed unduly or in the wrong way by modern psychology, explain the effect of a talisman as due entirely to suggestion. This is sheer nonsense. And

I can only assume that whoever makes this sort of argument is without the least experience of this type of magical work. It is this kind of experience which comprises or should comprise the first part of one's early practical work in the technical side of Magic. And lack of experience in even this elementary aspects of technical virtuosity vitiates every opinion on other forms.

We are confronted here by the same problem that arose over a century ago in another sphere. The early great magnetisers after Mesmer–great names like de Puysegur, Deleuze, du Potet and Lafontaine–claimed that by means of will and imagination they were able to open themselves to an influx from without and then to transmit from their own organisms a species of vital power or animal magnetism. This force pervading all space they claimed could be used therapeutically. Later on, when attempting to appropriate the trance phenomena and healing methods inaugurated by the mesmerists, physicians of the orthodox school eliminated the theory of an actual transmissible force and in its stead employed the theory of suggestion. Beginning with Braid and continuing through a line of very fine investigators, a duplication of magnetic phenomena was achieved purely by psychological means without recourse to any hypothesis of animal magnetism.

But because phenomena can be produced by one method does not necessarily imply that its duplication by another is false. It may well be that similar feats can be accomplished by quite separate techniques based upon differing hypotheses–each valid in its own sphere and each capable of explaining one set of facts. In any event, the reality of animal magnetism, or the transmission of what in the East has been termed *prana*, vitality, has never been disproved.

On the contrary, it is a simple matter to prove it quite adequate. Let any normal healthy person suspend his fingers over the arm of a second person, imagining and willing that his *prana* courses out from his fingers in long filmy streamers of energy. If the second person sits quite still and cultivates an objectivity of feeling and waiting, he will soon sense either a cold draught on that arm or a tingling in his own finger tips which proceeds from the influx of *prana*. This is an experience quite apart from suggestion, for it may be attempted with those who have no idea of the fundamental principles involved and who, therefore, are not directly susceptible to suggestion on this score. Spontaneously, and without prompting, they will observe the fact that a tangible transmission of vitality has been effected. It should be possible to test it by some very delicate instrument. Moreover, in a dark room, these streamers issuing from the fingers can be readily seen if the hand is held in front of a black cloth.

Furthermore, one's ability to generate this power is capable of culture. I have elaborated this theme from the point of view of autotherapy in *The Art of True Healing*. And it is also my suggestion that the interested reader consult Dr. Bernard Hollander's work *Hypnotism and Self-Hypnotism* where the problems of suggestion and animal magnetism are discussed at some length in connection with experimental work–and that most intelligently.

Briefly, let me say that suggestion does not invalidate in the least the fact of animal magnetism, nor the effect of a charged talisman. For, as I have intimated, we are confronted by the same problem that years earlier had arisen as to whether the trance and therapeutic phenomena of mesmerism were indeed due to suggestion or to a surcharge of vitality. If power can be passed on to an individual as I content it can, why not to some specific substance which is particularly appropriate in its nature to receiving a charge? Tradition has always asserted that metals, gems and precious stones, vellum and parchment make good materials bases for talismans. If the vitality of the operator be augmented by simple meditation exercises such as have been described in *The Art of True Healing*, or by the straightforward magical methods of invocation and visualisation of God-forms, then a very powerful charge is imparted to the material basis of the talisman.

Of itself, however, the talisman is nothing. It only becomes efficacious when properly consecrated and vitalised. Thus the Eucharistic substance is worthless as such until it has been duly consecrated by an appropriate magical ceremony, and transmuted into the vehicle of an appropriate type of force. The mode of consecration is of course, another matter, not to be described here inasmuch as it is a lengthy and technical business. One of the important parts of such a ceremony for the consecration of a talisman or a Eucharistic substance, is the assumption of the God-form astrally. When the operator has determined the nature of the divine force he is desirous to invoke, and having selected the material substance congruous in nature to that force, he must endeavour during his ceremony of consecration so to exalt the spirit within him that he actually becomes identified, in one way or another, with the consciousness of that particular force or deity. The more thorough and complete is this dynamic union, the more automatic and simple does the mere subsequent charging of the telesmata become. In the case of the Eucharist the idea, however, is not only spiritual identification with the deity as a preliminary to the ascent to the unknown universal God, but the glorified body. While the higher consciousness of the Magus may certainly be dissolve in ecstasy, it becomes imperative to create a magical link between that divine consciousness and his physical body and emotions. Therefore, the ceremonial magnetising of a material substance, be it a wafer or wine or herb, impregnates it with that same divine force. Its consumption assumes that transmuting force into the very being and fibre of the Magus, to carry out the work of transformation. As the pseudonymous Therion once wrote: "The magician becomes filled with God, fed upon God, intoxicated with God. Little by little his body will become purified by the internal lustration of God; day by day his mortal frame, shedding its earthly elements, will become in very truth the Temple of the Holy Ghost. Day by day matter is replaced by Spirit, the human by the divine; ultimately the change will be complete; God manifest in flesh will be his name."

It requires some little magical experience fully to appreciate this, but this simplified explanation will I think throw more light on the actual nature of the ceremony than does the description of Waddell.

I do not wish to discuss in more than a few words the validity of a Eucharistic ceremony celebrated other than by the operator himself. Bearing in mind that a properly performed Eucharistic ceremony results in the production of a talisman, it becomes clear that this kind of operation is principally of benefit to him who performs it. It seems to my way of thinking a useless rite to partake of the Eucharist *en bloc*. The Buddha is supposed to have remarked that no ceremonies are of the least avail in obtaining salvation or redemption. To me, it seems not that he attacked the magical tradition in these words, but rather wholesale ceremonies in which the audience plays no active part at all. There is no willed stimulation of their own spiritual principles–it is a passive vicarious participation in the labours of other people. Magic, with Buddhism, agrees with Madame Blavatsky's dictum that "the pivotal doctrine of the Esoteric philosophy admits no privileges or special gifts in man save those won by his own ego through personal effort and merit..."

There is one final topic I should like to refer to at some length before leaving this comparative study. In so doing it is necessary to leave Waddell for the moment to refer to the writings of two other Tibetan scholars, Madame Alexandra David Neel and Dr. W. Y. Evans Wentz. Both of these scholars have written with sympathy and understanding on Tibetan, religion and magical practices. The subject to be considered is a Tibetan mystery play in relation to Western magical ritual.

"*Chöd*" is a kind of mystery drama, and the magician or yogi is the sole actor therein. Dr. Evans Wentz, in his masterly introduction to the translation of the play or ritual in *Tibetan Yoga and Secret Doctrines* explains that the "*Chöd*" Rite is, first of all, a mystic drama, performed by a single human actor, assisted by numerous spiritual beings, visualised, or imagined, as being present in response to his magic invocation. Its stage setting is in some wild awe-inspiring locality, often in the midst of the snowy fastnesses of the Tibetan Himalayas, twelve to fifteen or more thousand feet above sea-level. Commonly by preference it is in a place where corpses are chopped to bits and given to the wolves and vultures. In the lower altitudes of Bhutan and Sikkim, a densely wooded jungle solitude may be chosen; but in countries wherein corpses are cremated, such as Nepal and India, a cremation-ground is favoured. Cemeteries or localities believed to be haunted by malignant and demonical spirits are always suitable.

"Long probationary periods of careful preparation under a master of *Chöd* are required before the novice is deemed fit or is allowed to perform the psychically dangerous rite...At the outset, the celebrant of the Chöd Rite is directed to visualise himself as being the Goddess of the All-Fulfilling (or All-Performing Wisdom) by whose occult will he is mystically empowered; and then, as he sounds the thigh-bone trumpet, invoking the gurus and the different orders of spiritual beings, he begins the ritual dance, with mind and energy entirely devoted to the one supreme end of realising, as the Mahayana teaches, that *Nirvana* and the *Sangsara* are, in reality, an inseparable unity.

"Stanzas three to seven inclusive suggest the profound symbolism underlying the ritual; and this symbolism, as will be seen, is dependent upon the Five Directions, the corresponding Five "Continents" of the *lamaic* cosmography with their geometrical shapes, the Five Passions (hatred, pride, lust, jealousy, stupidity) which the *yogin* triumphantly treads under foot in the form of demons, and the Five Wisdoms, the antidotes to the Five Passions...In the ninth stanza comes the dramatic spearing of the elements of Self with the spears of the Five Orders of *Dakinis*. As the Mystery proceeds, and the yogin prepares for the mystic sacrifice of his own fleshy form, there is revealed the real significance of the *Chöd* or 'cutting of.'

Thus the *Chöd* as explained by Evans Wentz is seen as a highly intricate magical ceremony in which the lama, identifying himself with a Goddess through the visualised assumption of her astral or ideal form, invokes what we in the West would call angels, spirits and elementals to attend upon his ceremony. These he deliberately invites to enter his own sphere of consciousness. Now he makes a vacuum as it were; he opens himself completely, and wholly receptive permits whatever influences will to permeate him through and through, and partake of his nature. In one sense, he sacrifices his being to them. His mind, his emotions and feelings, and the organs and limbs of his physical body, and the minute cells and lives composing them, are all handed over to the invaders for consumption, if so they wish. "For ages, in the course of renewed births I have borrowed from countless living beings–at the cost of their welfare and life–food, clothing, all kinds of services to sustain my body, to keep it joyful in comfort and to defend it against death. To-day, I pay my debt, offering for destruction this body which I have held so dear. I give my flesh to the hungry, my blood to the thirsty, my skin to clothe those who are naked, my bones as fuel to those who suffer from cold. I give my happiness to the unhappy ones. I give my breath to bring back the dying to life."

It is briefly, a very idealised form of personal sacrifice in which the wholly individuality is opened up, hypothetically, to whatever desires to possess it. As a magical operation it must rank very high in technical virtuosity, and for him who is sufficiently endowed with the magical gifts to perform it a most effectual ritual so far as results are concerned.

The final stage of the drama is ably described by Mme. David Need in this passage: "Now he must imagine that he has become a heap of charred human bones that emerges from a lake of black mud–the mud of misery, of moral defilement, and of harmful deeds to which he has co-operated during the course of numberless lives, whose origin is lost in the night of time. He must realise that the very idea of sacrifice is but an illusion, an offshoot of blind, groundless pride. In fact, he *has nothing* to give away, because he *is nothing*. These useless bones, symbolising the destruction of his phantom "I", may sink into the muddy lake, it will not matter. That silent renunciation of the ascetic who realizes that he holds nothing that he can renounce, and who utterly relinquishes the elation springing from the idea of sacrifice, closes the rite."

In attempting a comparison between this *Chöd* Rite and European magical rituals, we are at the outset confronted not by the problem of inferiority of conception or technical skill, as many have heretofore thought, but by a vast difference of metaphysical outlook. That is to say, there is a markedly enunciated opposition both of philosophic and pragmatic aim. In common with all schools and sects of Buddhism, the Mahayan is directly antagonistic to the ego idea. The whole of its philosophy and ethical code is directly concerned with the elimination of the "I" thinking. It holds that this is purely a fantasy bred of childish ignorance, very much as the mediaeval notion that the sun circumambulated the earth was the result of imperfect knowledge. Therefore the whole of its religious and philosophic scheme is directed towards uprooting this fantasy from the thinking of its disciples. This is the *Anatta* doctrine, and its importance to Buddhism is grounded in the belief that from this fantasy spring all sorrow and unhappiness.

European Magic, on the other hand, owes its fundamental doctrines to the Qabalah. Whilst having much in common with the broad outlines of Buddhism, the metaphysics of the Qabalah are essentially egocentric in a typically European way. Nevertheless, the terms of its philosophy are so general that they may be interpreted freely from a variety of angles. Whilst decrying the ills and limitations that accompany the false ego sense, it emphasises not so much the destruction of the ego as, with true Western practically, its purification and integration. It is a very useful instrument when it has been taught the needful lesson that it is not identical with the Self, but only one particular instrument, on small phase of activity comprised within the larger sphere of the total individual. Hence, the practical theurgy that arises as a superstructure from the basic theoretical Qabalah must also be affected by such a viewpoint. Instead of seeking to remove the ego as such, it seeks to extend the limited borders of its horizon, to enlarge its scope of activity, to improve its vision and its spiritual capacity. In a word so to enhance its psychological worth that in taking cognisance of the universal Self permeating all things, it may become identified with that Self. Here, then, is a fundamental distinction in the point of view envisaged.

Just as the "*Chöd*" has its roots in the primitive Bön animism of pre-Buddhistic Tibet, having been very clearly re-shaped by the Mahayanists, so the Western Ritual I propose to consider here also has a very crude origin. It dates possibly to the centuries immediately preceding our own Christian era. "The Bornless Ritual", which is the name it has come to be known by, may be found in its elementary form in Fragments of a *Graeco-Egyptian Work upon Magic*, published in 1852 for the Cambridge Antiquarian Society by Charles Wycliffe Goodwin, M.A. The ritual has since undergone considerable transformation. From a simple primitive prayer to ward off evil, in the hands of skillful theurgists trained in the Western tradition of the Golden Dawn, it has been evolved into a highly complex but most effectual and inspiring work. The Ritual, as such, now consists of a lengthy poem, five elemental invocations, and an eloquent peroration. Sandwiched between them is a Eucharistic ceremony.

In the prologue, the operator identifies himself with Osiris by means of the visualised assumption of the Egyptian God-form. That is to say, he formulates about him the form of Osiris. His imagination must be pictorially keen and vivid enough to visualise even the smallest details of dress and ornamentation in clear and bright colour and form. As a result of this effort, if he is successful, no longer is the ceremony conducted by a mere human being. On the contrary, the invocations and commands issue forth from the very mouth of God-head. Osiris in magical symbolism is human consciousness itself, when finally it has been purified, exalted, and integrated–the human ego as it stands in a balanced position between heaven and earth, reconciling and uniting both. In a Golden Dawn initiation ritual, one officer, whilst assuming: "I am Osiris, the Soul in twin aspect, united to the higher by purification, perfected by suffering, glorified through trial. I have come where the great Gods are, through the Power of the Mighty Name.

The lama, when performing the *Chöd* Rite, likewise imagines himself to be one of the *dakinis*, The Goddess of the All-Fulfilling Wisdom. She, so runs the interpretation of Madame Alexandra David Neel, represents esoterically the higher will of the lama. The concepts of both rituals actually are very similar.

But here the resemblance, superficial indeed, ends. For in the *Chöd* ritual the lama or hermit, invoking the various orders of demons and spirits, identifies them with his own vices and so sacrifices himself. He sees his ego comprised of hatred or wrath, pride, lust, jealousy and stupidity, and throws these qualities to the invading spirits and demons for consumption. He visualises his body as a corpse being dismembered by the wrathful goddess, and its organs also being preyed upon by a host of malignant entities. In a few words, a species of dissociation is intentionally induced.

Now in the Western system, the various orders of elementals are also invoked from their stations during this Bornless Ritual. But they are commanded to flow through the Magus with a view, not to preying upon him and thus destroying him, but to purify him. The intent is totally different. At each station or cardinal quarter, the appropriate tutelary deity is invoked by means of the formulation of the astral form and the proper lineal figures. In the East, as a result of the vibration of the appropriate barbarous names of evocation that "have a power ineffable in the sacred rites", and by enunciating the Words of Power, the Sylphs rush through his sphere of sensation like a gentle zephyr blowing the foul dust of pride before them. The Salamanders, raging from the South, consume with a burning fire the jealousy and hatred within him. Lust and passion become purified by the Undines invoked from the West, as though the Magus were immersed in purest water from which he issues spotless and consecrated. Whilst the Gnomes, coming from the North, cleanse him from sloth and stupidity, exactly as muddy and impure water is cleansed by being filtered through sand. The operator, all the while, is conscious of the injunction *a propos* the elementals given in one of his initiations. Or rather, the injunction has become a part of his unconscious outlook upon life. "Be thou, therefore, prompt and active as the Sylphs, but avoid frivolity and caprice. Be energetic and strong as the Salamanders but avoid irritability and ferocity. Be flexible and attentive to images like the Undines, but avoid idleness and changeability. Be laborious and patient like the Gnomes, but avoid grossness and avarice. So shalt thou gradually develop the powers of the thy soul, and fit thyself to command the spirits of the elements."

The elemental invocations over–very difficult work, to do which requires at least seventy or eighty minutes of intense magical concentration–the operator, being convinced of the presence of the invoked force and the salutary effect of their respective purifications upon him, begins the second stage of his work by invoking the fifth element, the alchemical quintessence, *Akasa* or the Ether, in both its negative and positive aspects. The effect of these two invocations is to equilibriate the elementals already commanded to the scene of operations. Also, it tends to provide an etheric mould or astral vacuum into which the higher spiritual forces may descend to make contact with the Unconscious psyche of the operator.

At this juncture it is customary to celebrate the mystic repast which again seems the reverse in intention of the *Chöd* banquet. At least, the reversal is only apparent. The Magus celebrates the Eucharist of the four elements, after reciting powerfully the Enochian invocation of the mystical Tablet of Union beginning *Ol Sonuf Vaorsagi goho Iada balta*–"I reign over you, saith the God of Justice..." The perfume of the rose on the altar, the low fire of the lighted lamp, the bread and salt, and the wine are thus powerfully charged with the divine force. So that as he partakes of the elements, the influx of the spirit elevates not only his own ego but all the innumerable cells and lives which comprise his own lower vehicles of manifestation. And more too, for it affects all the spiritual beings, angels, elementals, and spirits who, in answer to invocation, now pervade his astral sphere. Thus he accomplishes that which the tenets of all mystical religion enjoin, the elevation of all the inferior lives as man himself evolves. This he does, in this case, by the agency of the magical invocations and the Eucharist, so that not only does he himself become blessed by the impact of the divine spirit, but so do all the other beings present partake with him of the glory. There is no with-holding of blessing. For here, as in the *Chöd* Rite, there is no retention of power from any being.

At the opening of the ceremony, all forces and all beings whatsoever are carefully banished by the appropriate banishing rituals so as to leave a clean and holy space for the celebration of the ceremony. But into this consecrated sphere all the orders of elementals, comprised within the five-fold division of things, are called. And it is this mighty host who, having purified the sphere of the magus by having consumed the undesirable elements within him, are consecrated and blessed by the Eucharist and the descent of the refulgent Light. The whole operation is sealed by the peroration:

"I am He! The Bornless Spirit, having sight in the feet! Strong and the Immortal Fire! I am He the Truth! I am He who hate that evil should be wrought in the world! I am He that lighteneth and thundereth! I am He from whom is the shower of the life of earth! I am He whose mouth ever flameth! I am He, the Begetter and Manifester unto the Light! I am He, the Grace of the World! 'The Hearth girt with a Serpent' is my Name."

It coincides with the re-formation of the god-form of Osiris. And with each clause of the final hymn, the magician makes the effort in imagination to realise that they answer to the divine qualities and characteristics of the God, whose Light is even now descending upon him. The end result is illumination and ecstasy, a transporting of the consciousness of the magus to an identity with the consciousness of all that lives, an ineffable union with the Light, the One Life that permeates all space and time.

It will be conceded I hope that the Western conceptions of Magic are in no way inferior, as so many unfortunately have come in the past several years to believe, to those prevalent in Tibet and the East. It is only that the philosophic forms are somewhat different. And this difference has its roots in varying psychological needs–and these at no time are irreconcilable.

Here then I must content myself with these comparisons between various points of magical interest common to both East and West. My desire to compare them sprang originally from a perusal of Major Waddell's really erudite book–where the reader may find other items of great and absorbing interest. But I do feel that unless he has the magical key to these practices and various ceremonies which the Lamas perform, he is apt to be bored and left without a proper understanding of them. With all due respect to the Eastern wisdom for which assuredly I have a great and profound reverence, it is my belief that in this instance a study of Theurgy as developed by Western genius is more capable than aught else of throwing an illuminating ray on the true nature of spiritual development by means of the path of Magic. There are many paths to the one goal of the Beatific Vision. Of these paths, meditation is one. Probably in its development of meditation and the purely introspective processes of Yoga, the East is far in advance of the West. Certainly there is no better text-book on that subject than the Patanjali Yoga Aphorisms. And I appreciate the fact that Blavatsky brought Theosophy from the East. But Theurgy has climbed to sun-illuminated heights in the Western Schools. Our hidden sanctuaries of initiation, where Magic has long been successfully employed, but all too rigidly suppressed from the notice of the outer world, have a finer, nobler and more spiritual interpretation than any to be found in Eastern systems.

For myself, I can only say that experience demonstrates that Theurgy makes no confusion in its statement of ideals. It introduces no superstitious chaos concerning the fear of demons, etc., which is only too apparent in the Tibetan scheme, judging from Waddell's book. Every magical effort of the Lamas is described as being due to fear or hatred of evil spirits, though I do not doubt but that many lamas have a finer understanding of their system than this. Theurgy nurtures the ideal that its technique is a means of furthering one's spiritual development so that thereby one may consummate the true objects of incarnation. Not selfishly, but that one may be the better able thereafter to help and participate in the ordered progress of mankind to that perfect day when the glory of this world passes, and the Sun of Wisdom shall have arisen to shine over the splendid sea.

THE ART OF MAGIC

Of all the subjects which comprise what nowadays is called Occultism, the most misunderstood of all is Magic. Even Alchemy, which to some of us is annoyingly dark and obscure, evokes far more sympathy and understanding as a rule than does Magic. For example, the psychologist Jung has observed of alchemy in his essay *The Ego and The Unconscious* that "it would be an unpardonable depreciation of value if we were to accept the current view, and reduce the spiritual striving of the alchemists to the level of the retort and the smelting furnace. Certainly this aspect belonged to it; it represented the tentative beginnings of exact chemistry. But it also had a spiritual side which has never yet been given its true value, and which from the psychological standpoint must not be underestimated." Yet Magic, strange to say, receives no such evaluation–except insofar as the term Magic is allied to the unconscious, and is said to represent a primitive attempt to cognise the Unconscious. There is, hence, hardly more than the barest minimum attempt to arrive at an understanding of its processes.

For the moment, I do not wish to analyse the possible reasons for this amazing phenomenon. What is more to the point, however, is to provide some more or less intelligible approach to the subject so that given an initial glimpse of the bright light flooding the world of Magic, more people may feel disposed to devote just a little of their energies and time to its study. The advantages and benefits are such as to make this effort extremely worth while.

Putting it simply and briefly, let me say at the outset that Magic concerns itself in the main with that self-same world as does modern psychology. That is to say, it deals with that sphere of the psyche of which normally we are not conscious but which exerts an enormous influence upon our lives. Magic is a series of psychological techniques so devised as to enable us to probe more deeply into ourselves. To what end? First, that we shall understand ourselves more completely. Apart from the fact that such self-knowledge in itself is desirable, an understanding of the inner nature releases us from unconscious compulsions and motivations and confers a mastery over life. Second, that we may the more fully express that inner self in every-day activities. It is only when mankind as a whole has reached, or perhaps when the more advanced men and women in the world have evolved, some degree of inner realisation that we may ever hope for that ideal utopian condition of things–a wide tolerance, peace, and universal brotherhood. It is to ends such as these that Magic owes its *raison d'etre*.

Approaching the matter from another point of view, it may be said that Magic deals with the same problems as Religion. It does not waste its or our valuable time with futile speculations with regard to the existence or nature of God. It affirms dogmatically that there is an omnipresent and eternal life principle–and thereupon, in true scientific fashion, lays down a host of methods for proving it for oneself. How may we know God? Here, as before, there is a well-defined and elaborate technique for dealing with the human consciousness as such and exalting it to an immediate experience of the universal spirit permeating and sustaining all things. I say advisedly that its technique is well-defined. For the system has an abhorrence of the attitude of those good-natured but muddle-headed thinkers who, refusing to accept their human limitations as they are now, aim too high without dealing with the manifold problems in the way.

Let us assume that yonder building is ten storeys high. How may we reach the roof? Certainly not by ignoring the very obvious fact that at least two hundred feet intervene between us and the roof! Yet that is precisely the attitude of the so-called simplicity cult in mystical religion. God they affirm, is an exalted state of infinite consciousness to which the microcosmic mind must be united. So far, so good—and here Magic is in accord with their view. Therefore, these people propose to attempt gaining the summit of attainment by ignoring the steps between man as we find him now and the supreme end—God. It is as though they wished to jump from the ground to the roof of the aforesaid building.

Magic adopts a slightly different attitude. It is one, however, which is markedly similar to the common-sense attitude of the mystical man in the street. To get to the top of the building we must either climb the various flights of stairs leading there, or else take the lift upwards. In either case, it is a graduated process—an evolution, if you wish.

Man, holds the magical theory, is a more or less complicated creature whose several faculties of feeling, sensation, and thinking have slowly been evolved in the course of aeons of evolution. It is fatal to ignore these faculties, for evidently they were evolved for some useful purpose in answer to some inner need. Hence, in aspiring towards divine union, surely a laudable goal, we must be quite sure that our method, whatever it is, takes unto consideration those faculties and develops them to the stage where they too may participate in the experience. If evolution is held up as a suitable process, then the whole man must evolve, and not simply little bits or aspects of him, whilst other parts of his nature are left undeveloped at a primitive or infantile level of being. Moreover, these faculties must be so trained as to be able to "take" the enormous tension sure to be imposed upon them by so exalted but nevertheless so powerful an attainment. Each faculty must be deliberately trained and carried stage by stage through various levels of human and cosmic consciousness so that gradually they become accustomed to the high potential of energy, ideation, and inspiration that must inevitably accompany illumination and an extension of consciousness. Failure to consider such a viewpoint in terms of its dynamics undoubtedly must account for the catastrophes so frequently encountered in occult and mystical circles.

To present a bird's-eye view of the entire field of Magic, let me summarily state that for convenience the subject may be divided into at least three major divisions. One–Divination. Two–Evocation and Vision. Three–Invocation. I will define each separately and at some little length.

With regard to the first division, the magical hypothesis is quite definite. It holds that divination is not ultimately concerned with mere fortune-telling– nor even with divining the spiritual causes in the background of material events, though this latter is of no little importance. On the contrary, however, the practice of divination when conducted aright has as its objective the development of the inner psychic faculty of intuition. It is an enormous asset spiritually to have development of the inner psychic faculty of intuition. It is an enormous asset spiritually to have developed an exquisite sensitivity to the inner subtle world of the psyche. When carried on for a sufficiently long period of time, the practice builds slowly but efficiently a species of bridge between the consciousness of man and that deeper hidden part of his psyche of which usually he is not aware–the Unconsciousness, or higher Self. In these deeper spiritual aspects of his nature are the divine roots of discrimination, spiritual discernment, and lofty wisdom. The object of divination is quite simply, then, the construction of a psychic mechanism whereby this source of inspiration and life may be made accessible to the ordinary consciousness, to the ego. That this mechanism is concerned at the outset with providing answers to apparently trivial questions is by itself no objection to the technique itself. The preliminary approaches to any study may seem unworthy to or incompatible with that study. And divination is no exception to the general trend. Nor is the objection valid that the technique is open to frequent abuse by unscrupulous charlatans. But practised sincerely and intelligently and assiduously by the real student, consciousness gradually opens itself to a deeper level of awareness.

"The brain becomes porous to the recollections and dictates of the soul," to use a current theosophical expressions, is a true statement of the actual results of the training. As the statement of the actual results of the training. As the object of analytical psychology is the assimilation of the repressed content of the Unconsciousness to the ordinary wake-a-day consciousness, so by these other magical means the human mind becomes aware of itself as infinitely vaster, deeper and wiser than ever it realised before. A sense of the spiritual aspect of things dawns upon the mind–a sense of one's own innate high wisdom, and a recognition of divinity working through man and the universe. Surely such a viewpoint elevates divination above the level of a mere occult art to an intrinsic part of mystical endeavor.

Geomancy, Tarot and Astrology, these are the fundamental techniques of the divinatory system. Geomancy is divination by means of earth. At one time, its practitioners actually used sand or black earth in which to trace its sigils and symbols–a typically primitive or mediaeval method. Today Geomantic diviners use pencil and paper, relying upon graphite in their pencils to formulate, theoretically, a magical link between themselves and the so-called divining intelligences or elementals of Earth. It is, so far as my own experience goes, a highly efficient technique, and I can claim at least an 80% degree of accuracy over several years. Tarot is the name of a set of cards, seventy-eight in number, which were introduced into Europe in either the fourteenth or fifteenth century from...? No-one knows where they came from. Their origin is a complete mystery. At one period in Europe there were no such cards available, so far as we can see. At another time, the cards available, so far as we can see. At another time, the cards were circulating freely. Little mention need be made of astrology, since that has long been one of the most popular methods with which the public has been made familiar. Anyone who practises these methods with this objective in mind will assuredly become aware of the results I have described. And while, it is true, his querents for divination may receive perfectly good answers to the questions they have asked, departing from his threshold in the spirit of gratitude and wonder, the intuitive development accruing to him will constitute the more important side of that transaction.

It is when we leave the relatively simple realm of divination to approach the obscure subject of Evocation that we enter deep waters. Here it is that most difficulty has arisen. And it is in connection with this phase of Magic that the greatest misunderstanding and fear even has developed.

In order to elucidate the matter, let me again turn to the terminology of modern psychology. The term "complex" has achieved a fairly wide notoriety during the last quarter of a century since the circulation of the theories of Freud and Jung. It means an aggregation or group of ideas in the mind with a strong emotional charge, capable of influencing conscious thought and behavior. If my interest is Magic, then naturally every item of information acquired, no matter what its nature, is likely to be built by association into that constellation of ideas clustering around my interest–becoming in the course of years a thoroughgoing complex. Mrs. Jones my dairy-woman, because of her professional predilection, will have her complex centering about milk and cows and butter and the price of eggs.

Over and above this definition, however, is the more subtle one of a group of ideas or feelings congregating about a significant or dominant psychic theme, such as sex or the need to overcome inferior feelings, or some psychic wound of childhood, tying or locking up nervous energy. Thus, as a result of repression, we may find a complex of which the possessor is totally unconscious–a complex expressing itself in a sense of insecurity, obsession by morbid unreasonable fears, and persistent anxiety. Moreover, a constellation of feelings and moods and emotional reactions may exist which have become so powerful and yet so obnoxious to reason as to have become completely split off from the main stream of the personality. What modern psychology calls a complex in this sense, the ancient psychology of Magic, which had its own system of classification was the Qabalistic Sephiros or the ten fundamental categories of thought.

Thus, should we essay translation of terms, the sense of inferiority we might call the spirit of *Tipharas*, whose name is said to be *Soras*, inasmuch as the Sun, one of its attributions or associations, is considered the planetary symbol of the individuality. Hence an affliction to the personality, which may be considered a general or rough definition of the inferiority sense, could well be referred to *Soras*–since the spirit in the case of each Sephirah is considered evil. That complex expressing itself in insecurity is the spirit of *Yesod* and the Moon, whose name is *Chashodai*. This sphere of *Yesod* represents the astral design or foundation imparting stability and permanence to physical shapes and forms; in a word it is a symbol of security and strength. Should we be confronted with a case where the emotions were split off from consciousness–this is the influence of the spirit of *Hod* and Mercury, *Taphthartharath*. One wallowing in emotional chaos, having refused to develop equally consciousness–this is the influence of the spirit of *Hod* and Mercury, *Taphthartharath*. One wallowing in emotional chaos, having refused to develop equally consciousness and the rational faculties, is subject to the spirit of *Netsach* and Venus, *Haniel*. A purely destructive or suicidal neurosis which causes one to exhibit the symptomatic tendency deliberately to break things, or to use them in attack against oneself, is of a martial quality, belonging to *Gevurah* and Mars, the spirit *Samael*.

This, naturally, is the subjective point of view. That there is a purely objective occult theory I do not deny, but that cannot be dealt with here.

How, nowadays, do we deal with the psycho-neuroses in the attempt to cure them–to eliminate them from the sphere of the patient's thinking and feeling? Principally by the analytical method. We encourage the patient to narrate freely his life-history, to delineate in detail his early experiences in connection with his father and mother, his reactions to brothers and sisters, to school and playmates and the entire environment. He is asked to dwell particularly on his emotional reaction to these earlier experiences, to relive them in his imagination, to recount and analyse his feelings towards them. Moreover, his dreams at the time of analysis are subjected to a careful scrutiny. This is necessary because the dream is a spontaneous psychic activity uninterfered with by the waking consciousness. Such activity reveals present-day unconscious reactions to the stimuli of life–reactions which modify, even form his conscious outlook. In this way the patient is enabled to realise *objectively* the nature of this complex. He must detach himself from it for a short space of time. And this critical objective examination of it, this understanding of its nature and the means whereby it came into being, enables him, not once and for all, but gradually and with the passage of time, to oust it from his ways of thinking.

Magic, however, at one time proceeded according to a slightly different technique. It to realised how devastating were these natural but perverse ways of thinking, and how crippling was the effect they exercised on the personality. Indecision, vacillation, incapacitation of memory, anaesthesia of feeling and sense, compulsions and phobias, besides of host of physical and moral ills, are the resultants of these complexes or spirit-dominants. So completely is the patient at the mercy of obsessing moods as almost to be besides himself, thus suggesting to the vivid imagination of the ancients an actual obsession by some extraneous spirit entity. So, in order to restore man to his former efficiency, or to the standard of normality, these afflictions must be eliminated from consciousness.

As its first step, Magic proceeded to personalise them, to invest them with tangible shape and form, and to give them a definite name and quality. It is the nature of the psyche spontaneously to give human characteristics and nomenclature to the contents of its own mind. In doing this, the magical system receives the official blessing, if I may say so, of no less a modern psychological authority than Dr. C. G. Jung. In his commentary to *The Secret of the Golden Flower*, Jung names these complexes "autonomous partial systems." Referring to these partial systems, he asserts: "Being also constituents of the psychic personality, they necessarily have the character of persons. Such partial-systems appear in mental diseases where there is no psychogenic splitting of the personality (double personality), and also, quite commonly, in mediumistic phenomena." It is, as I have said, a natural tendency of the human mind to personalise these complexes or groupings of special ideas. As another proof of this, we may cite the phenomenon of dreams, in which quite frequently the patient's psychic difficulties or complexes are given symbolically some human or animal form.

Proceeding a step further, the ancient science of Magic postulated that to eliminate this complex it was necessary to render it objective to the patient's or student's consciousness so that he might acquire some recognition of its presence. Whilst these subconscious knots of emotion, or astral spirits, are unknown and uncontrolled, the patient is unable to control them to the best advantage, the patient is unable to control them to the best advantage, to examine them thoroughly, to accept the one or to reject the other. First of all, was the hypothesis, they must acquire tangible, objective form before they may be controlled. So long as they remain intangible and amorphous and unperceived by the ego, they cannot adequately be dealt with. By a programme of formal evocation, however, the spirits of the dark underworld, or complexes of ideas inhabiting the deeper strata of unconsciousness, may be evoked from the gloom into visible appearance in the magical triangle of manifestation. Evoked in this technical way, they may be controlled by means of the transcendental symbols and formal processes of Magic, being brought within the dominion of the stimulated will and consciousness of the theurgist. In other words, they are once more assimilated into consciousness. No longer are they independent spirits roaming in the astral world, or partial systems dwelling in the Unconscious, disrupting the individual's conscious life. They are brought back once more into the personality, where they become useful citizens so to speak, integral parts of the psyche, instead of outlaws and gangsters, grievous and dangerous enemies threatening psychic unity and integrity.

How are these evoked? What is the technical process of rendering objective these autonomous partial-systems? Magic parts company here with orthodox psychology. Many months of tedious analysis at enormous financial outlay are required by the present-day psychological method to deal with these problems, and few there be who are strong enough or patient enough to persist. The magical theory prefers a drastic form of emotional and mental excitation by means of a ceremonial technique. During the Evocation ceremony, divine and spirit names are continuously vibrated as part of a lengthy conjuration. Circumambulations are performed from symbolic positions in the temple–these representing different strata of the unconscious, different regions of the psychic world. Breath is inhaled into the lungs, and, rather like the pranayama technique of the Hindu Yogis, manipulated by the imagination in special ways. By means of these exercises, consciousness is stimulated to such a degree as to become opened, despite itself, to the enforced upwelling of the content of the Unconscious. The upwelling is not haphazard but is definitely controlled and regulated. For the Qabalists were thoroughly familiar with the ideas of suggestion and association, arranging their conjurations so that by means of association of ideas there would be suggested to the psyche the train of ideas required–and only that train of ideas required—and only that train. The particular partial-system is then exuded from the sphere of sensation and projected outwards. It embodies itself in so-called astral or etheric substance normally comprising the interior body which serves as the foundation or design of the physical form, and acting as the bridge between the body and the mind, of which it is the vehicle. The astral form now reflecting the partial-system projected from the Unconscious, attracts to itself particles of heavy incense burned copiously during the ceremony. Gradually, in the course of the ceremonial, a materialism is built up which has the shape and character of an autonomous being. It can be spoken to and it can speak. Likewise it can be directed and controlled by the operator of the ceremony. At the conclusion of the operation, it is absorbed deliberately and consciously back into the operator by the usual formula. "And now I say unto thee, depart from hence with the blessing of (the appropriate divine name governing that particular type of complex) upon thee. And let there ever be peace between me and thee. And be thou ever ready to come and obey my will, whether it be a ceremony or but by a gesture."

Thus the defect in consciousness caused by the spirit-obsession is remedied and, because of the accession to consciousness of the tremendous power and feeling involved in such a repression, the psyche of the operator is stimulated in a special way, according to the nature of the spirit. To recapitulate, the purpose of Evocation is that some portion of the human psyche which has become deficient in a more or less important quality is made intentionally to stand out, as it were. Given body and name by the power of the stimulated will and imagination and exuded astral substance, it is, to continue to use metaphor, specially nourished by the warmth and sustenance of the sun, and given water and food that it may grow and flourish.

Familiarity, of course, is requisite before this type of Magic should be attempted. It requires study and long training. Arduous and persistent toil needs to be undertaken with the appropriate formulae before one dare apply oneself to so formidable and perhaps dangerous an aspect of the magical routine. But it has this advantage over the analytical procedure. It is infinitely speedier when once the technique has been mastered and the special association tracks have been familiarised, and considerably more thorough and effective as a cathartic agent. I hope one day to see a modification of it in current use by our psychologists.

There is an important variation of this technique. At first sight, it may seem to bear but little relationship with the Evocation method. But it too has as its objective the necessary assimilation of the unconscious content of the psyche into normal consciousness. Its object, also, is the enlarging of the horizon of the mind by enlarging the student's intellectual conceptions of the nature of the universe.

The elementary technical processes of this method call for the drawing or the painting of coloured symbols of the elements Earth, Air, Water, Fire and Ether. Each of these has a different traditional symbol and colour. To Earth is attributed a yellow square. Air is a blue circle. Water is a silver crescent. Fire, the red triangle, and Ether is the black egg. After staring intently at the symbol of some one particular element for several seconds, and then throwing the vision to some white or neutral surface, a reflex image of the complementary colour is seen against it. This is a normal optical illusion without having in itself any special significance. The optical reflex obtained, the student is counselled to close the eyes, *imagining* that before him is the symbolic shape and complementary colour of the element being used. The shape is then to be enlarged until it seems tall enough for him to visualise himself walking through it. Then he must permit the fantasy faculty of the mind full and unimpeded play. What is particularly important is that at this stage he must vibrate certain divine and archangelic names which tradition ascribes to that particular

In "The Art of Magic" the Tattvas described are illustrated in colour. The Divine and Archangelic Names referred to as being listed in "*The Golden Dawn*" are as follows:

EARTH:	yellow square	ADONAI HA ARETZ	AURIEL
AIR:	blue circle	SHADDAI EL CHAI	RAPHAEL
WATER:	silver crescent	ELOHIM TZABAOTH	GABRIEL
FIRE:	red triangle	JEHOVAH TZABAOTH	MICHAEL
ETHER:	black oval	EHEIEH	YEHESHUAH

It should be noted that this is one particular tradition and that other practitioners may use alternative correspondences. In the illustration below, white is used instead of silver with regard to the crescent because this is found to give easier results and the optical reflex will be found to be silver.

symbol. These names may be found in the first volume of my work The Golden Dawn.

In this way, he enters imaginatively or clairvoyantly by means of a vision, into the elemental realm corresponding to the nature of the symbol he has chosen. By employing element after element, he acquires a sympathetic contact with the understanding of the several hierarchical planes existing within Nature, and thus widens tremendously the sphere of his consciousness.

From the psychological point of view, we might understand the magical theory to imply that the Unconscious (which has been compared to the nine-tenths of an iceberg concealed under water and not at all visible) may be classified into five principal layers of sub-divisions. These five levels correspond to the five elements, the most superficial being Earth, and the deepest being Ether or Spirit. By following such a vision or fantasy technique the candidate's ordinary consciousness is enable to cross the otherwise impenetrable barrier subsisting between it and the unconscious. A link is formed between the two aspects of mind, a bridge is constructed, across which the psyche may pass at any moment. Entering these various psychic levels by way of an association track by means of which idea, inspiration, and vitality are made available to consciousness.

The vision thus obtained corresponds generally to a sort of dream, experienced however in a fully conscious state—one in which none of the faculties of consciousness, such as will, criticism and keen perception are in any way in abeyance. The goal of analysis, from the synthetic and constructive point of view, is accomplished readily by such means. A wide range of knowledge and feeling is thereby opened up and assimilated without strain or difficulty to the advantage and spiritual development of the individual.

Interpretation of the vision is an important factor. The neglect of interpretation may account for the intellectual sterility and spiritual emptiness so frequently observed in those who employ similar methods. Acquaintance with the methods of Jung's symbolic analysis of dreams and spontaneous fantasies may be extremely useful here, providing a useful adjunct to the Qabalistic reference of symbols to the ten Sephiros of the Tree of Life. Before passing on, it is interesting to note that Jung gives towards the end of his book *Two Essays on Analytical Psychology* an account of a patient's spontaneous fantasy which is curiously similar to the tattwa technique I have just described. He calls it a " 'vision' which by intense concentration was perceived on the background of consciousness, a technique that is perfected only after long practices." It is so interesting that I am constrained to quote it here: "I climbed the mountain and came to a place where I saw seven red stones in front of me, seven on either side, and seven behind me. I stood in the middle of this quadrangle. The stones were flat like steps. I tried to lift the four stones that were nearest to me. In doing so I discovered that these stones were nearest to me. In doing so I discovered that these stones were the pedestals of four statues of gods which were buried upside down in the earth. I dug them up and so arranged them around me that I stood in the middle of them. Suddenly they leaned towards one another so that their heads touched, forming something like a tent over me. I myself fell to the earth, and said, 'Fall upon me if you must, for I am tired.' Then I saw that beyond, encircling the four gods, a ring of flame had formed. After a time I arose from the ground and overthrew the statues of the gods. Where they fell to the earth four trees began to grow. And now from the circle of fire blue flames shot up which began to burn the foliage of the trees. Seeing this I said 'This must stop. I must go into the fire myself so that the leaves may not be burned.' Then I stepped into the fire. The trees disappointed and the ring of fire contracted to one immense blue flame that carried me up from the earth."

Divination, Evocation and Vision are the preliminary techniques of Magic. We have observed that there is considerable justification for their employment—when there is adequate understanding of their meaning and technical procedure. But these are preliminary methods only. They are but steps leading to the consummation of the supreme sacrament. The inevitable end of Magic is identical to that conceived of in Mysticism, union with God-head. Magic conceives of divinity as Spirit and Light and Love, It is an all-pervasive and omnipresent vital force, permeating all things, sustaining every life from the most minute electron to the largest nebula of mind-staggering dimensions. It is this Life which is the substratum of the entirety of existence, and it is this primal consciousness in which we live and move and have our being. In the course of manifestation, cosmic centres develop within its infinitude, centres of lofty intelligence and power, whereby the cosmic high tension may be modified and reduced to a lower key so as ultimately to produce an objective manifestation. These cosmic centres of life are what for the moment we may name the Gods (not spirits)—beings of enormous wisdom, power and spirituality in an ascending hierarchical scale between us and the unknown and unnamed God. The particular hierarchy that they form receives in Magic a clear classification in terms of the Qabalistic Tree of Life.

In an earlier paragraph I gave the metaphor of a man striving to reach the roof top of a several storeyed building. Now Magic conceives of spiritual development in an analogous way. That is to say, it conceives a personal evolution as progressive and orderly. Divinity is the objective we seek to reach, the roof top. We, those of us cherishing the mystical ideal, are below on the ground. Not with one leap may we attain the summit. An interviewing distance demands to be traversed. To reach the roof we must use either stairs or lift. By means of the magical technique we employ the invocation of the Gods, who answer metaphorically to the stairs or lift, and attempt union with their wider and vaster consciousness. Since they represent the several cosmic levels of energy and mind intervening between us an the supreme goal, as we unite ourselves in love and reverence and surrender to them, so much the nearer do we approach to the ultimate source and root of all things.

Using the plan of the Tree of Life as his guide, the magician invokes the lower Gods or Archangels as they are named in another system, desirous of mingling his own life with, and surrendering his own being to, the greater and more extensive life of the God. Thus his spiritual perceptions become finer and more sensitive, and his consciousness becomes with time accustomed to the high tension of the divine force flowing through him. His interior evolution proceeding, he invokes the God of the Sephirah or plane immediately above. Following the same procedure, he attempts to assimilate his own essence, his own integrated consciousness, to that of the divinity he has invoked. And so on–until finally he stands upon the lofty Darien peak of spiritual realisation, united with the transcendental life of infinity, feeling with universal love and compassion, conscious of all life and every thing as himself with supreme vision and power. As Iamblichus, the Neoplatonic theurgist, once expressed it: "If the essence and perfection of all good are comprehended in the gods, and the first and ancient power of them is with is priests (i.e. theurgists or magicians) and if by those who similarly adhere to more excellent natures and genuinely obtain a union with them, the beginning and end of all good is earnestly pursued; if this be the case, here the contemplation of truth, and the possession of intellectual science are to be found. And a knowledge of the Gods is accompanied with...the knowledge of ourselves."

So much for theory. How does the art of invocation proceed? Most important of all is the imaginative faculty. This must be trained to visualise symbols and images with the utmost clarity, ease, and precision. The necessity for this springs from the fact that certain God-forms are to be visualised. Most popular in magical techniques are the Egyptian God-forms. There seems to be a certain quality of specific definiteness about forms such as Osiris, Isis, Horus and Nuit, for example, which renders them peculiarly effective for this kind of training. In another system, where the Archangels are synonymous with the divine Gods, forms are visualised based upon an analysis of the individual letters comprising of God-name. That is to say, should we employ the Jewish Qabalistic system, each Hebrew letter has attributed to it a colour, astrological symbol, divinatory meaning in Tarot and Geomancy, and element. When building up the so-called Telesmatic image of the Archangel in the imagination, we take each letter as representing some particular part or limb of the Form, and some particular shape, feature, or colour. Thus from the letters of its name, a highly significant and eloquent form is ideally constructed.

Seated or lying in a perfectly relaxed state, one in which no muscular or nervous tension can send a disturbing message to the brain, the student endeavors to imagine that a particular God-form or Telesmatic Image surrounds him or coincides with his physical shape. Sometimes but a few minutes suffice to produce a conscious realisation of the presence, though more often than not a good hour's work at the least is required to procure worthwhile results. As concentration and reflection become more intense and profound, the body becomes vitalised by streams of dynamic energy and power. The mind, too, is invaded by Light, great intensity of feeling, and inspiration.

The name of the God or Archangel is meanwhile frequently vibrated. This vibration serves two ends. One, to keep the mind well concentrated on the ideal form by means of repetition. Two, the vibration awakens in the depths of the microcosmic consciousness that magical faculty which is akin or corresponds to its macrocosmic power. Rhythmic breathing likewise is undertaken so as to tranquilise mind and body, and to open the subtler parts of the inner nature of the omnipresent all-permeating life. Visualisations of the letters of the Name moreover are practised. According to traditional rules, the letters are manipulated by the mind as moving within the forms, or occupying certain important positions on plexuses or major nerve centres. The totality of these methods conspire to exalt the consciousness of the operator, to lift up his mind by no devious or uncertain route to a nobler interior plane where is a perception of the meaning and transcendental nature and being of the God.

Over and above all these methods, or, more accurately, combining these techniques, is a final phase of Magic which I propose only to touch upon in brief— Initiation. The necessity and rationale of this process depends upon the postulated ability of a trained initiate to impart something of his own illumination and spiritual power to a candidate by means of a ceremony. Such a magnetic transmission of power is conceived to stir up the inner faculties of the candidate–faculties dormant and obscured for many a sorry year. As Psellus, another Neoplatonist once remarked of Magic, "Its function is to initiate or perfect the human soul by the power of materials here on earth, for the supreme faculty of the soul cannot by its own guidance aspire to the sublimest intuitions, and to the comprehension of Divinity."

Since the divine principles of man are obscured and latent within him, so that consciousness, of itself and by itself is unable to climb to the distant heights of spiritual intimacy with universal life, Magic in the hands of a trained and experienced Magus is the means whereby that eclipse of the inner light may be overcome. By means of several initiations, the seeds of awakening are sown within the soul. Later they are fanned and stimulated into an active living flame lighting the brain, illuminating the soul, and providing the necessary guidance to accomplish the purpose of incarnation.

The number of ceremonies and their detailed implication must differ, naturally, with different systems, though in general meaning all are in complete accord. In one system of initiation which is of especial significance to me personally, the major initiation ceremonies are seven in number. The first of these is a ceremony of preparation, consecration and purification, bringing to the dull gaze of the neophyte some vague intimation of the Light to which he aspires and which seems lost in the dim darkness afar. The seed of the Light is sown deeply within him by way of suggestions embodied in ritual speeches so that, time and devotion to the work acting as incubating agents, it may grow and blossom into the full-grown tree of illumination and divine union. The next five ceremonies are concerned with developing what are termed the elemental bases of the soul. Consciousness, placed under the surveillance of the Light, requires to be strengthened in its elemental aspects. So that when the Light ultimately does indwell the soul of man, the elemental self may be strong enough and pure enough to support the soul so that it may safely bear the full brunt of the divine glory. At first, this may not appear perhaps an urgent necessity. But if one remembers the pathologies of mysticism, the well-meaning but scatter-brained and unpractical people of this world who have been totally unfitted for the conquest of life by a mild species of psycho-spiritual experience, then the magical routine obtains some degree of justification. It is in vain that the wine of the gods is poured into old cracked vessels. We must make certain that the vessels are intact and strong, capable of retaining and not spilling the wine poured from above.

The five elemental ceremonies having been experienced, and the seeds of the divine Earth, Air, Water, Fire and Ether sown within the human soul, the candidate is ready for the final initiation of this particular series. The central point of this initiation is the invocation of what commonly is called the higher Self, or the Holy Guardian Angel. This is the central core of the individuality, the root of the Unconscious. Before union with the Infinite may be envisaged, it is necessary that every principle in the human constitution be united so that man becomes one united consciousness, and not a disconnected series of separate discrete consciousness. The intelligence of the physical cells comprising the body, the principle of the emotions and feelings, the sphere of the mind itself, these must be united and bound together by a conscious realisation of the true nature of the Self employing them, the higher Genius. Integrity produced through the agency of the telestic or initiatory rites, then the whole human being, the entire man may set forth upon that lengthy but incomparable bright road which leads to the end, and to the beginning also, of life. Then, and only then, is man able to realise the meaning of life, and the purpose of his multitudinous incarnations on earth. No longer is a vague mysticism countenanced and idealised as a cowardly escape from the difficulties and turmoils of this life. With these latter he is now capable of dealing and, moreover, of completely mastering them, so that no longer do they enslave him. By no ties either of attachment or disgust is he bound to the duties of this earth–ties which must necessitate his further and continued incarnation until he has successfully severed them.

Freedom obtained through the acquisition of integrity in its truest and divinest sense, then the next magical step in evolution is possible of recognition and achievement–the conscious return of man to the divine Light from which he came.

THE MEANING OF MAGIC

We live today in a world of great material progress and mechanical ingenuity. On every hand is flouted the social advantages of the world-wide communication bequeathed to us by such modern inventions as aviation, radio and space-craft. Time seems to disappear in the face of such things, and space dwindles almost to nothing. The peoples of the earth are drawn far closer together than ever they have been before in recorded history. By the way of paradox, however, simultaneously with this unique advance in scientific progress, a large proportion of mankind is supremely miserable. It suffers the pangs of dire starvation because scientific methods have yielded an over-production of foods and manufactured articles without having solved the problem of distribution. Yet modern science has become invested with a nature which originally was not its own. Despite the chaos of international affairs, and the fear of another catastrophic war present in the minds of most people, it has become robed in a mighty grandeur, almost of divinity. Perhaps it is because of this feeling of insecurity and fear that this condition has come about, for the human psyche is a cowardly thing at core. We cannot bear to be honest with ourselves, accepting the idea that whilst we are human we are bound to feel insecurity, anxiety and inferiority. Instead, we project these fears outwards upon life, and invest science or any body of knowledge with vast potential of affect so as to bolster up our dwindling fund of courage. So science has become, thanks to our projected affect, an authority that hardly dares to be questioned. We cannot bear that it should be questioned for we must feel that in this subject at least is authority, unshakable knowledge and the security we so dearly crave. The phenomenon is hardly dissimilar to that of a few centuries ago when religion, formal religion of the churches, was the recipient of this obeisance and respect. For many people, science has now become their intellectual keynote, by whose measuring rod–despite their own personal neuroses and moral defects–all things soever are ruled, accepted or rejected.

Pursuits no matter of what nature which temporarily are not popularly favored, even though in them lies the hope for the spiritual advancement of the world, or subjects which do not possess the sanction of those who are the leading lights in the scientific world, are apt thus to receive as their lot neglect and gross misunderstanding. When many folk are introduced to Magic, for instance, the first reaction is either one of stark fear and horror–or else we are greeted by a smile of the utmost condescension. This is followed by the retort intended to be devastating that Magic is synonymous with superstition, that long ago were its tenets exploded, and that moreover it is unscientific. This, I believe, is the experience of the majority of people whose prime interest is Magic or what now passes as Occultism. It seems that just as their hope for security and their desire for unshakable knowledge becomes projected upon science, so their inner fears and unfaced terrors are projected upon this maltreated body of traditional knowledge, Magic. Disconcerting this reaction can most certainly be, unless criticism and the call for definitions immediately is resorted to. By these means alone may we who champion Magic obtain a begrudged hearing.

Science is a word meaning knowledge. Hence any body of knowledge, regardless of its character– whether ancient mediaeval, or modern–is a science. Technically, however, the word is reserved primarily to imply that kind of knowledge reduced to systematic order. This order is encompassed by means of accurate observation experimentally carried out over a period of time, the classification of the behaviour of natural phenomena alone, and the deduction of general laws to explain and to account for that behaviour. If this be the case, then Magic must likewise claim inclusion within the scope of the same term. For the content of Magic has been observed, recorded and described in no uncertain terms over a great period of time. And though its phenomena are other than physical, being almost exclusively psychological in their effect, they are of course natural. General laws, too, have been evolved to account for and explain its phenomena.

A definition of Magic presents a rather more difficult task. A short definition which will really explain its nature and describe the field of its operation seems practically impossible. One dictionary defines it as "the art of applying natural causes to produce surprising effects." Havelock Ellis has ventured the suggestion that a magical act is a name which may well be given to cover every conceivable act in the whole of life's span. It is Aleister Crowley's suggestion that "Magic is the science and art of causing changes to occur in confronting with will." Dion Fortune slightly modified this by adding a couple of words—"changes in consciousness." The anonymous mediaeval author of *The Goetia, or Lesser Key of King Solomon* has written a proem to that book where occurs the passage that "Magic is the highest, most absolute, and most divine knowledge of Natural philosophy...

True agents being applied to proper patients strange and admirable effects will thereby be produced. Whence magicians are profound and diligent searchers into Nature."

Have these definitions taught us anything of a precise nature about the subject? Personally I doubt it very much; all are too general in their scope to tend towards edification. Let us therefore cease seeking definitions and consider first of all certain aspects of fundamental principles of the subject. Afterwards, perhaps, we may have sufficient trustworthy and evidential material at our disposal to formulate anew a definition which may convey something intelligible and precise to our minds.

Within the significance of the one term Magic are comprehended several quite independent techniques, as I shall mention on a later page, in another essay. It may be advantageous to examine some of these techniques. Before doing so, however, it might be well to consider a part of the underlying theory. I know many will say by way of criticism of this discussion, that it is nothing but primitive psychology–and only the psychology of auto-suggestion at that. There will be a decided sneer, barely concealed.

However, this objection does not completely dispose of the subject by any means. A very great deal more remains to be said. Not that I would deny that in

Magic the process of self-suggestion is absent. Most certainly it is present. But what I must emphasize here is the fact that it is present is a highly evolved and elaborate form. It almost makes the technical approach of some of our modern experimenters look puerile and undeveloped. We are not to suppose for one moment that the innovators and developers of the magical processes in days gone by were naive or fools, unaware of human psychology and the structure of the mind itself. Nor that they refrained from facing many of the psychic problems with which we nowadays have had to deal. Many of the early magicians were wise and skilled men, artists and sages, well-versed in the ways and means of influencing and affecting people.

We know that they understood a good deal about hypnotism and the induction of hypnoidal states. It is highly probable that they speculated, as have done innumerable modern psychologists, upon technical methods of inducing hypnoidal states without the aid and help a second person. But they soon became aware of all the obstacles and barriers that beset their path. And these were many. I believe that in Magic they devised a highly efficient technical procedure for overcoming these difficulties.

When Coué some years ago burst upon our started horizon with his spectacular formula of "day by day in every way I am getting better and better" many believed that here at last we were presented with the ideal method of getting down to brass tacks, of finally being able to impinge upon the Unconscious mind, so called. Hundreds of thousands of people surely must have gone to bed at night, determined to induce a relaxation that was as nearly perfect as they could obtain, and attempted to enter the land of slumber while muttering sleepily the magical formula over and over again. Others listened to music in dimly lighted rooms until they experienced some sense of exaltation and then mumbled the healing phrase until they felt that surely some favourable result must occur.

Assuredly some lucky people got results. They were, however, few and far between. Some of these did overcome certain physical handicaps of illness, nervousness, so-called defects in speech and other mannerisms, and thus were able to better themselves and their positions in the world of reality. Others were less fortunate–and these were by far the greater number, the great majority.

What was the difficulty that prevented these people, this large majority, from applying the magical formula until success was theirs? Why were they not able to penetrate that veil stretched between the various levels of their minds.

Before we answer these questions–and I believe that Magic does really answer them–let us analyze the situation a little more closely.

The unconscious in these systems of so-called practical psychology, metaphysics, and auto-suggestion, is considered a slumbering giant. These systems hold that it is a veritable storehouse of power and energy. It controls every function of the body every moment of every day, nor does it sleep or tire. The heart beats seventy two times per minute, and every three or four seconds our lungs will breathe in oxygen and exhale carbonic acid and other waste products. The intricate and complex process of digestion and assimilation of food which becomes part and parcel of our very being, the circulation of blood, the growth, development and multiplication of cells, the organic resistance to infection–all these processes are conceived of as immediately under the control of this portion of our minds of which we are not normally aware–the Unconscious.

This is only one theoretical approach to the Unconscious. There are other definitions of its nature and function which altogether preclude the practical possibility of resorting to suggestion or auto-suggestion for coping with our ills. For example, there is the definition provided by Jung with which in many ways I am in sympathy, and it might be worth our while to quote it at some length.

He wrote in *Modern Man in Search of a Soul* that "man's unconscious likewise contains all the patterns of life and behaviour inherited from his ancestors, so that every human child, prior to consciousness, is possessed of a potential system of adapting psychic functioning...While consciousness is intensive and concentrated, it is transient and is directed upon the immediate present and the immediate field of attention; moreover, it has access only to material that represents one individual's experience stretching over a few decades...But matters stand very differently with the unconscious. It is not concentrated and intensive, but shades off into obscurity; it is highly extensive and can juxtapose the most heterogeneous elements in the most paradoxical way. More than this, it contains, besides an indeterminable number of subliminal perceptions, an immense fund of accumulated inheritance-factors left by one generation of men after another, whose mere existence marks a step in the differentiation of the species. If it were permissible to personify the unconscious, we might call it a collective human being combining the characteristics of both sexes, transcending youth and age, birth and death, and, from having at his command a human experience of one or two million years, almost immortal. If such a being existed, he would be exalted above all temporal change; the present would mean neither more nor less to him than any year in the one hundredth century before Christ; he would be a dreamer of age-old dreams and, owing to his immeasurable experience, he would be an incomparable prognosticator. He would have lived countless times over the life of the individual, of the family, tribe and people, and he would possess the living sense of the rhythm of growth, flowering and decay."

Granted this kind of definition, the whole idea of suggesting ideas to this "dreamer of age-old dreams" sounds utterly presumptuous. Only a simpleton, living a superficial intellectual and spiritual life, would have the audacity to dare give this "being" suggestions relative to business, marriage, or health. Such a concept then immediately rules out the use of suggestion, demanding more sophisticated approaches.

For the time being, and only for the purpose of this discussion, let us grant validity to the first concept of the unconscious as being a titan who will respond to suggestions if the latter can be gotten through to him. The theory goes, therefore, that if, in the face of some bodily ill or disfunction, we could literally *tell* the Unconscious what we want done, these results could occur in answer to our concentrated wish. Theoretically, the theory sounds all right. Unfortunately, for one thing, it does not take into consideration the fact that early in life an impenetrable barrier is erected within the psyche itself. A barrier of inhibition is built up between the unconscious and the conscious thinking self–a barrier of prejudices, false moral concepts, infantile notions, pride and egotism. So profound is this armoured barrier that our best attempts to get past it, around it, or through it are utterly impotent. We become cut off from our roots, and have no power, no ability, to contact the deeper, the instinctual, the more potent side of our natures.

The various schools of auto-suggestion and metaphysics all have different theories and techniques with regard to overcoming this barrier. That some people do succeed is unquestionable. One meets almost every day an individual here and there who is able to "demonstrate"–to use the ghastly word they so glibly employ. These few are able to impress their Unconscious minds with certain ideas which fall as though upon fertile soil, fructify and bring salutary results. These we cannot deny–much as sometimes we would like to, so offensive is their smugness, their dogmatic attitude, their unthinkingness.

But by far the great majority of their devotees fail lamentably. They have not obviously been able to overcome this difficulty by the employment of the usual routines.

I am sure the ancient sages and magi knew of these problems–knew them very well. I am also quite sure that they realized that the technique they used was, amongst other things, a process of suggesting a series of creative ideas to themselves. But what I am equally certain of is this. They had perfected an almost ideal method which proved itself able to penetrate this hitherto impenetrable endopsychic barrier. They were able to reach this imprisoned titan locked up in the hearts of every one of us, and set it free so that it could work with them and for them. Thus they became almost lyrical in their descriptions of what could not be accomplished by the individual who employed their techniques with courage and perseverance.

As I say, they knew of the existence of this psychic armoring, and knew it only too well. All their methods were directed to mobilizing all the forces of the individual, reinforcing his will and imagination, to the end that he could overcome himself to realize his kinship, his identity and unity with the unconscious self.

What these methods were, I hope to describe in some small detail in these pages. Some of them may appear irrational to us. They certainly are irrational. But that is no argument for rejecting them summarily. A great part of life itself *is* irrational. But it is incumbent upon us to accept life in all its aspects, rational and irrational as well. One of the very earliest things a psycho-analytic patient learns is this one fact–that he has at least two sides to his nature, a rational and an irrational side. Together they comprise a single discrete self, his personality. If he denies the validity or existence of either one of them, he does violence to himself and must suffer accordingly. Both of these two factors must be permitted to exist side by side, the one affecting the other. In this way, the individual grows, intellectually, emotionally and spiritually, and all his ways will prosper. With denial, nothing but trouble, neurosis and disease can follow.

These irrational processes that were instituted of old as the technique of Magic comprise the use of invocation or prayer, of the use of the imagination in formulating images and symbols, of employing the religious sense to awaken ecstasy and an intensity of feeling, of rates of breathing that would alter the accustomed neuro-physiological patterns and so render more permeable the barrier within the mind itself. Everything that would conduce to a heightening of feeling and imagination, that would lead to the instigation of an overpowering ecstasy, would be encouraged, for it would be in this psychological state that the normal barriers and confines of the conscious personality could be over-ridden in a tempestuous storm of emotional concentration.

It was the ancient theory that the unconscious or the deeper levels of the psyche could be reached principally by two methods. These were intense concentration, and intensity of emotion. The former is extremely difficult of achievement. Certainly there are methods whereby the mind itself may be trained so to concentrate that eventually a funnel, as it were, is created by the mind, through which suggestions could be poured into the unconscious to work their way out in the way out in the various ways desired. But such methods are for the very few. There is only an individual here and there who has the patience and the indomitable will to sit by himself for a certain period during the day, and each day, and subject himself to an iron mental discipline.

The emotional intensity, while not easy to cultivate, at least is more within the bounds and possibilities of achievement than is the other. It was this method that the ancient magicians cultivated to a very fine art. They devised innumerable means whereby the normal physiological habits could be changed and altered, so as to permit of this impingement upon the underlying basis of the self.

To summarise, there is Divination, the art of obtaining at a moment's notice any required type of information regarding the outcome of certain actions or events. Fortun tell so-called is an abuse. The sole purpose of the art is to develop the intuitive faculties of the student to such an extent that eventually all technical methods of divination may be discarded. When that stage of development has been reached, mere reflection upon any problem will automatically evoke from the intuitive mechanism within the information required, with a degree of certainty and assurance involved that could never be acquired save from an inner psychic source.

Another phase–perhaps that which has been stressed more than all others–is Ceremonial Magic in its widest sense. Comprised within this expression, are at least three distinct types of ceremonial endeavour, all, however, subject to one general set of rules or governed by one major formula. The word "ceremonial" includes rituals for initiation, for the invocation of Gods so-called, and the evocation of elemental and planetary spirits. There is also the enormous sphere of talismans, and their consecration and charging. Ceremonial is probably the most ideal of all methods for spiritual development since it entails the analysis and subsequent stimulation of every individual faculty and power. Its results are genius and spiritual illumination. But personal aptitude is so potent a factor in this matter, as well as in divination, that although the word "Art" may be applied to cover their operation it would be unjust to Magic to denominate it a Science.

The third, and in some ways the most important branch for my particular purpose at the moment, is Vision, or the Body of Light technique. It is with this latter that I shall deal exclusively in this essay, as it contains elements which I feel answer more definitely to the requirements of a Science than any other.

In discussing Magic, the reader's pardon must be sought if reference is continually made to a technical philosophical system named the Qabalah. They are so interlaced that it is well-nigh impossible to separate them. Qabalah is theory and philosophy. On the other hand, Magic is the practical application of that theory. In the Qabalah is a geometrical glyph named the Tree of Life, which is really a symbolic map both of the universe in its major aspects, and of it microcosm, man. Upon this map are depicted ten principal continents, so to say, or ten fields of activity where the forces constituting or underlying the Universe function in their respective ways. In man these are analysable into ten facets of consciousness, ten modes of spiritual activity. These are called the Sephiros. I cannot enter more fully into an outline of this map here though I have repeatedly referred to it here and in other essays; but the reader will find it adequately described in various books or articles on the subject.

Now consider with me that especial Sephirah or subtle aspect of the universe called by the Qabalists *Yesod*. Translated as the sphere of the Foundation,

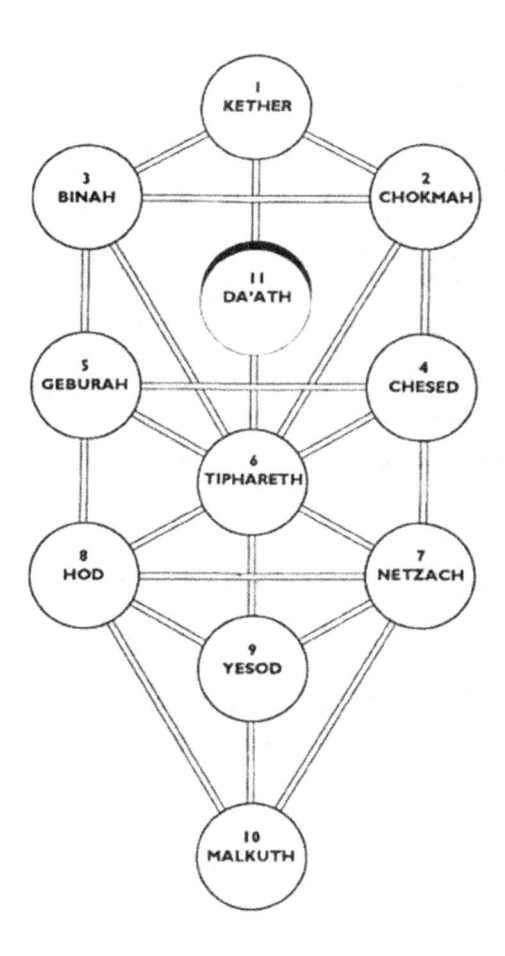

The Tree of Life

it is part of the Astral Light—an omniform plane of magnetic, electric, and ubiquitous substance, interpenetrating and underlying the whole of the visible perceptible world. It acts as a more or less permanent mould whereupon the physical world is constructed, its own activity and constant change ensuring the stability of this world as a compensating factor. In this world function the dynamics of feeling, desire and emotion, and just as the activities of this physical world are engineered through the modalities of heat and cold, compression and diffusion, etc., so in the astral are operative attraction and repulsion, love and hate. Another of its functions is to exist as the memory of nature, wherein are automatically and instantaneously recorded every act of man and every phenomenon of the universe from time immemorial to the present day. The nineteenth century Magis, Eliphas Levi, has written of this astral Light that: "There exists an agent which is natural and divine, material and spiritual, a universal plastic mediator, a common receptacle of the vibrations of motion and the images of forms, a fluid and a force, which may be called in some way the Imagination of Nature…" And again he registers the conviction that is "the mysterious force whose equilibrium is social life, progress, civilization, and whose disturbance is anarchy, revolution, barbarism, from whose chaos a new equilibrium at length evolves, the cosmos of a new order, when another dove has brooded over the blackened and distributed waters."

It is interesting to glance from this theurgic concept to a psychological one which is not very unlike it. The following paragraph is more or less of a paraphrase of Jung's ideas concerning it, culled from an essay of his entitled *Analytical Psychology and Weltanschauung*. It is an extension of the ideas previously quoted. He defines it first of all as the all-controlling deposit of ancestral experience from untold millions of years, the echo of prehistoric world-events to which each century adds an infinitesimally small amount of variation and differentiation. Because it is in the last analysis a deposition of world-events finding expression in brain and sympathetic nerve structure, it means in its totality a sort of timeless world-image, with a certain aspect of eternity opposed to our momentary, conscious image of the world. It has an energy peculiar to itself, independent of consciousness, by means of which effects are produced in the psyche that influence us all the more powerfully from the dark regions within. These influences remain invisible to everyone who has failed to subject the transient world-image to adequate criticism, and who is therefore still hidden from himself. That the world has not only an outer, but an inner aspect. That it is not only an outer, but an inner aspect. That it is not only outwardly visible, but also acts powerfully upon us in a timeless present, from the deepest and most subjective hinterland of the psyche–this Jung holds to be a form of knowledge which, regardless of the fact that it is ancient wisdom, deserves to be evaluated as a new factor in forming a philosophic world-view. I suggest, then, that what the Magicians imply by the Astral Light is identical in the last resort with the Collective Unconscious of modern psychology.

By means of the traditional Theurgic technique it is possible to contact consciously this plane, to experience its life and influence, converse with its elemental and angelic inhabitants so-called, and return here to normal consciousness with complete awareness and memory of that experience. This, naturally requires training. But so does every department of science. Intensive preparation is demanded to fit one for critical observation, to provide one with the particular scientific alphabet required for its study, and to acquaint one with the researches of one's predecessors in that realm. No less should be expected without due preparation. Anyone with even the slightest visual imagination may be so trained as to handle in but a short while the elementary magical technique, by which one is enabled to explore the subtler aspects of life and the universe. To transcend this "many-coloured world." To gain admittance to loftier realms of soul and spirit is quite another matter. One calling for other faculties and other powers, particularly a fiery devotion and an intense aspiration to the highest.

But with the latter, I am not just now concerned, even though it is the pulsing heart and more important aspect of Theurgy. It is with the scientific aspect of Magic, its more readily verifiable aspect, that I shall deal now. Elsewhere I have given as traditional attributions or associations to the sphere in question the following symbols. Its planet is said to be the Moon, its element Air, its number Nine, its colour purple– and also silver in another scale. The Pearl and Moonstone are its jewels, aloes it perfume, and its so-called divine name is *Shaddai El Chai*. The Archangel attributed to it is Gabriel, its choir of Angels are the four Kerubs ruling the elements, and its geomantic symbols are Populus and Via. The Tarot of the four suits numbered IX, and closely associated with it also is the twenty-first trump card entitled "The World." Here we find depicted a female form surrounded by a green garland. Actually this trump card is attributed to the thirty-second path of Saturn which connects the material plain to *Yesod*. How, now, arises the question, how were these symbols and names obtained? What is their origin? And why are they so called attributions or correspondences of that Sephirah called the Foundation?

First of all, meditation will disclose the fact that all have a natural harmony and affinity one with the other—though not perhaps readily seen at the first glance. For example, the Moon is, to us, the fastest moving planet. It travels through all the twelve signs of the zodiac in about twenty-eight days. The idea of rapid change is there implicit, revealing the concept that the astral, while almost a timeless eternal deposit of world events, is nevertheless the origin of mutations and altercations which later influence the physical world—in the same way that impulse and thought must precede any action. Its element is air, a subtle all pervading medium—comparable to the astral light itself—a medium without which life is quite impossible. Nine is the end of all numbers, containing the preceding numbers within its own sum. It always remains itself when added to itself or multiplied, or subtracted, suggesting the fundamental all-inclusive self-sustaining nature of the realm.

What is still more important, however, from the scientific viewpoint is that they are things, names, and symbols actually perceived in that sphere by the skryer in the spirit-vision. As a matter of solid proof, one could quote numerous visions and astral journeys obtained by different people in different places at different times, in which all the traditional symbols appear in dynamic and in curiously dramatic and vital form.

Magic, as already remarked, is a practical system, and every part has been devised for experiment. Each part is capable of verification using appropriate methods. Each student may check it for himself, and thus discover the realities of his own divine nature as well as of the universe both within and without him, independently of what any other man may have written in books. We ask for experiment; demand it even, for the sake of mankind. We invite the earnest and sincere student to experiment for himself with that technique described in Chapter Ten of my book *The Tree of Life*, and then compare his results, the journey to any one Path or Sephirah, with the correspondences briefly delineated in my other work *A Garden of Pomegranates* or in Dion Fortune's book *The Mystical Qabalah*. It is with the utmost confidence that I say one hundred astral journeys obtained in that way will correspond in *every* instance with the major symbols, names, numbers and ideas recorded in the several books of the Qabalah.

Let me quote from the record of a colleague an illuminating passage or two illustrating what I mean. The following is a "vision" or waking dream–fantasy of the so-called thirty-second path. "We marched down the wide indigo road. There was a cloudy night-sky–no stars. The road was raised above the general level of the ground. There was a canal each side beyond which we could see the lights of what appeared to be a large city. We went on like this for a long way, but then I noticed in the distance a tiny figure of a woman, like a miniature–she seemed to be naked, but as she drew near, I saw a scarf floating round her. She had a crown of stars on her head and in her hands were two wands. She came towards us very quickly, and I gazed fascinatingly at a string of pearls reaching from her neck to her knees–and gazing, found that we had passed through the circle of her pearls, and she had disappeared.

The student of the Qabalah who has only a passing acquaintance with Tarot symbolism, will recognize here the twenty-first Atu of "The World," the path attributed to Saturn, linking the physical to the astral worlds. He will probably be very surprised to learn that the symbols on these cards represent dynamic and exceedingly vital realities. But I must pass on to a brief description of the entrance to *Yesod*.

"Now the sky is clear and full of stars...The Moon, a great yellow harvest moon, rises slowly up the sky to a full arch...and we saw the moonbeams shining on the high purple walls of a city...We did not delay to look about, but marched quickly to the centre of the city, to an open space, in the midst of which was a round temple like a ball of silver. It was approached by nine steps, and rested on a silver platform. It had four doors. Before each was a large angel with silver wings...Inside, we were in a very airy place. Light breezes lifted our clothes and our hair–the interior was very white and clear silvery–no colours. Suspended in the centre was a great globe, like the moon itself... While we looked we saw that the globe was not suspended in the air; it rested on immense cupped hands. We followed the arms up and saw, far up near the roof, deep dark eyes looking down, dark like the night sky. And a voice said..."

Little point would be gained to continue with the rest of the quotation. This passage is given here soley that the reader may refer to the description of the astral plane in the textbooks, and then to the recurrence in this vision of the major symbols, and the dynamic form of dramatization. Let the student take good notice of the presence of the correct numbers, colours, planetary attributions, and above all the hint as to how much valuable knowledge may be acquired. Note the four doors to the Temple–representing the four major elements of fire, water, air and earth. For this astral world is also referred to the Ether (of which the element Air is a surrogate), the fifth element, quintessentialising the lower elements, the Temple to which the other elements are but doors. Suspended in the centre of the temple was a globe, symbolic possibly of the element of Air itself which, in the Hindu Tattwa system, is represented by a blue sphere. Before each of the doors stands an angel. These are the four Kerubic Angels, the vice-regents of the four cardinal quarters and elements ruling over a particular elemental world under the dominance of one of the letters of the Tetragrammaton. Possibly they are representations of the interior psychic delimitation of the soul's spatial area, so to speak, the absence of which would indicate an unhealthy diffusion or de-centralization of consciousness. Also the four cardinal points of space would be represented by these four angelic figures—concretizations, too, of the double play of the moral opposites. East is opposite to west, and north opposite to south, whilst each of these quarters has attributed to it some particular moral quality or psychic function. The sense of being in an airy place with light breezes bears out the formal attribution of fair—a curious confirmation of the duality of meaning implied in *pneuma*, wind and spirit, a duality which occurs not only in the Greek, but in Hebrew, Arabic, and a host of primitive languages.

Individual after individual has been trained independently to visit this and other Sephiros. While each vision is somewhat different in its detail and form to that here quoted, nevertheless there is a startling unanimity so far as concerns the essential symbolic features. This constitutes definite scientific proof of the supreme reality of the world of Magic, and demonstrates the possibility of personal experiment and research. Scientific research is possible in this world of astral or Unconscious realities, because they are effective things, that is, objective influences that work and influence mankind. This sphere is the deposit of the world experience of all times, and it is therefore an image of the world that has been forming for aeons, an image in which certain features, the so-called dominants, have been elaborated through the course of time. These dominants are the ruling powers, the gods and archangels and angels–that is representations of dominating laws and principles functioning in the brain structure and sympathetic nervous system of every individual it is a world which is open to every one who wishes to overcome the fear which centuries of mal-education have projected upon it, and discover for himself anew the reality of its dynamic urges and influences.

With but little ingenuity, specific tests may be undertaken with the object of testing the relationship between geometrical symbols, the vision obtained therefrom by means of the body of light technique, and the correspondences of these figures recorded in the proper books. It has been written that various elements– Fire, Water, Spirit, Air, and Earth–are attributed to the five points of the Pentagram. Depending entirely on the direction in which the lines are traced, so will the figure invoke or banish the beings pertaining to that element. For example, if the student traces the invoking Pentagram of Fire in each of the four cardinal quarters, and then employs the sensitive sight of the Body of Light which previously he has cultivated, he will see appear almost immediately the fire elementals or Salamanders, the personalized fiery constituents of his own psyche. The tracing of the banishing fire pentagram will see them literally scuttle away without hesitation, subsiding into the Unconscious realm to which they belong, and from which they were called. Or let the student do this experiment in the presence of a reliable clairvoyant, not mentioning what figure is being traced. The results will be highly illuminating. I know some objection may be raised by immediately responding "telepathy". But so far as I can see, the response arouses far more obscure problems than the rationale to which objection is made, for telepathy certainly requires explanation along scientific and dependable lines, quite difficult at this stage of the game. These and a host of other rigorous tests constitute definite and precise scientific experiment of a significant and highly authoritative nature.

In the sense that several people may travel to certain paths and there undergo experiences wherein the essential features are identical or in which the psychic dominants coincide. Magic may be assumed to be a definite, coherent science. It is precise and accurate. Magic is the accumulated record of psychic and spiritual experience which we have inherited from the past, from former generations of mankind.

On the other hand, it is clear that each of these visions would differ materially as to context, that is in the dramatic sense. The context, act and scene so to speak, depend entirely upon personal idiosyncrasy, intellectual integrity, and the spiritual capacity to discover and absorb the truth, whether it is painful to the ego or not. Where the personal element enters so powerfully as it does here, the adventure must be labelled an Art. Creative imagination in one person will be used to formulate with an established conventional set of symbols a whole string of incidents and experiences–illuminating and tending to the expansion of his consciousness–which to the vision of a simple unimaginative person would occur in far simpler and matter-of-fact form.

Sophisticated people, with a smattering of modern psychology, are like to assume that Magic discloses nothing but the hidden depths of the Unconscious. The will say that these journeys are comparable to dream experiences which are referred to the working and dramatizing power of the subconscious mind. What difference does it make if the Qabalist named this sphere or type of consciousness the Foundation or Astral World and the moderns the Unconscious?

The terms are cognate, and the symbols interchangeable; both mean the same thing, when all things are considered. If Magic possesses weapons that are more penetrating and incisive than scientific ones, shall we reject them because Magic is the discredited house where they are stored? If magical methods reveal our secret selves more directly, and unlock the vast store of wisdom and power within our souls, showing us how to control them in ways that neither psycho-analysis nor any modern science has succeeded to do, should we not be foolish to reject its benefits?

Magic is a scientific method. It is a valid technique. Its approach to the universe and the secret of life's meaning is a legitimate one. If it assists us to become more familiar with what we *really* are, it is a Science–and a most important one. And to the scientist, whether he be psychologist or physicist, it will open up an entirely new universe of tremendous extent. If it succeeds in making us better men and women, a little more kind and generous, a little more aware of the spiritual heights to which we are capable of climbing with but a little exertions, then it is the religion of religions. And should it spur us to greater efforts in order to render life and living more beautiful and intelligible, should it make us more anxious to eliminate ugliness, suffering, and ignoble misery, surely it is an Art before which all other Muses must bow the head and bend the knee in reverential and perennial praise!

BIBLIOGRAPHICAL NOTE

In "Magic in East and West" the magical techniques referred to are dealt with in some detail in *Magical Ritual Methods* by W. G. Gray.

In "The Meaning of Magic" the technique referred to as appearing in *The Tree of Life* Chapter 10 is described by Gareth Knight in a contribution to *The New Dimensions Red Book* edited by B. L. Wilby. The Correspondences mentioned as being in *A Garden of Pomegranates* are also described in detail in *A Practical Guide to Qabalistic Symbolism* by Gareth Knight and the subject is also dealt with in *The Ladder of Lights* by W. G. Gray.

New Falcon Publications
**Publisher of Controversial Books and CDs
Invites You to Visit Our Website:
http://www.newfalcon.com**

At the Falcon website you can:

- Browse the online catalog of all our great titles, including books by Robert Anton Wilson, Christopher S. Hyatt, Israel Regardie, Aleister Crowley, Timothy Leary, Osho, Lon Milo DuQuette and many more
- Find out what's available and what's out of stock
- Get special discounts
- Order our titles through our secure online server
- Find products not available anywhere else including:
    - One of a kind and limited availability products
    - Special packages
    - Special pricing
- And much, much more

Get online today at http://www.newfalcon.com